DISCARD

P9-CCV-199

Newark Public Library
Newark, New York 14513

Caboose

Mike Schafer

Motorbooks International
Publishers & Wholesalers ®

First published in 1997 by Motorbooks International Publishers & Wholesalers, PO Box 1, 729 Prospect Avenue, Osceola, WI 54020 USA

© Andover Junction Publications, 1997

All rights reserved. With the exception of quoting brief passages for the purpose of review no part of this publication may be reproduced without prior written permission from the Publisher

Motorbooks International is a certified trademark, registered with the United States Patent Office

The information in this book is true and complete to the best of our knowledge. All recommendations are made without any guarantee on the part of the author or Publisher, who also disclaim any liability incurred in connection with the use of this data or specific details

We recognize that some words, model names and designations, for example, mentioned herein are the property of the trademark holder. We use them for identification purposes only. This is not an official publication

Motorbooks International books are also available at discounts in bulk quantity for industrial or sales-promotional use. For details write to Special Sales Manager at the Publisher's address

Library of Congress Cataloging-in-Publication Data Available

ISBN 0-7603-0376-2

On the front cover: A fresh coat of red paint belies the real age of this classic caboose of the Chicago, Burlington & Quincy, shown tagging along at the rear of the "Oregon (Illinois) Turn," a local freight that is in the siding at Rochelle, Illinois, to make way for the Seattle-bound *Empire Builder* passenger train. Though looking virtually new, this "waycar"—as cabooses were called on the Burlington—had been built well over a half century earlier. *Mike Schafer*

On the frontispiece: Northern California's Mount Shasta—two miles high and then some—makes for an imposing backdrop for this Southern Pacific freight winding its way down the road's Siskiyou Line toward Sacramento, California, in April 1990. Cabooses were still a way of life on many SP trains. *Brian Solomon*

On the title page: The calm grandeur of the Columbia River is briefly ruffled by the passing of an eastbound Burlington Northern freight en route from Portland, Oregon, to Spokane, Washington, in the spring of 1972. The bright red caboose belongs to BN predecessor Spokane, Portland & Seattle and will some day be repainted into BN green. *Mike Schafer*

On the back cover: Out of the tunnel and into history: A Delaware & Hudson train, still equipped with a caboose, heads out of Factoryville Tunnel in eastern Pennsylvania. *C. W. Newton*

Printed in Hong Kong

CONTENTS

ACKNOWLEDGMENTS

O.K. So my name is in lights on the cover of this book. But that doesn't mean I did *everything*. Rarely, if ever, are book projects done entirely by one person, even if only one person is listed as the author.

Behind the scenes, I had lots of help. ("You *need* help," my cohorts say, "for choosing a vocation that keeps you and your Macintosh burning the midnight oil.") First of all, I wish to thank my associates—whom also double as close friends—within our company, Andover Junction Publications, the producer of this book. So, Joyce Mooney, thank you as always for your unfailing moral support, and thank you Steve Esposito for helping with the research (and additional moral support).

But those aren't the only friends who came to my call for help. I would also like to thank Chet and Sandy French for sharing their home during my visits to prod Chet's memories of his 35-year-plus railroad career, and thanks must go to Mike McBride as well for his critique of the manuscript and aid in research.

Neighbor Guy Kieckhefer, who I think knows more about railroad freight cars than anyone I know, was instrumental in providing much resource material, and Brian Solomon, former editor of *Pacific RailNews* magazine, proved as helpful as ever on various captioning questions.

And, of course, the book would not be possible without the folks at Motorbooks International, publisher of this book. Thank yous to Jack Savage, Keith Mathiowetz, and others at MBI for doing the final transformation of putting manuscript and photos into book form.

Mike Schafer

Cabooses were once as much a part of the American scene as wooden barns, yellow schoolbuses, and neon-clad dairy bars. Every town and city that boasted a railroad was visited at least once a day by a freight train and its caboose. In this scene dated July 10, 1965, Illinois Central Railroad's daily way freight on the Clinton-Freeport (Illinois) line calls at Dixon in the sleepy heat of late afternoon. While the station agent prepares waybills inside the 1800s-era brick depot, the train waits to resume its northward journey. Blue sky, fluffy clouds, and a red caboose indicate that all is right with the world. *Mike McBride*

INTRODUCTION

They were once as much an American institution as A&W root beer stands, Woolworth "five & dimes," and Harley-Davidson motorcycles. Cabooses have been an integral part of the North American railroading scene since about the mid-nineteenth century when railways became firmly entrenched on U.S. soil.

Cabooses quickly became a familiar sight to countless folks who encountered trains during their daily routines. And to thousands of conductors and brakemen, the caboose became almost as familiar as their own homes—for reasons explained shortly.

And just exactly what is the purpose of a caboose? The answer is pretty simple. Think of a freight train as a sort of warehouse on the move. A 75-car freight could easily contain millions of dollars worth of merchandise, manufactured components, fresh produce, and bulk commodities (coal, stone, iron ore pellets, etc.). To move this warehouse, you have a locomotive or a set of locomotives manned—and nowadays often womanned—by a crew. So you see, a train is very much a business unto itself. And for this business and its crew you need a boss . . . and that boss—on the railroad, that's the train conductor—needs an office from which to monitor the business and the crew. Voila! The caboose. It's a train's office.

But the caboose could be other things, too. It also served as a sort of storehouse and shop, and for over-the-road train crews, the caboose could also become a home away from home. The caboose's storehouse/shop aspect was reflected by the provisions within: spare coupler parts, jacks and rerailing devices, oil, first-aid kit, lanterns, and fuses. The crew could thus be able to handle at least the routine problems of getting a train over the road. And as homes? Well into the post-World War II era, it was common for specific cabooses to be assigned to specific conductors. At the end of the crew's run—even if the train were continuing beyond—the caboose with its crew was uncoupled from the train and parked. Instant motel.

The caboose population peaked in the late 1920s—the height of railroading's Golden Era—when more than 25,000 "crummies" (their most common nickname) were registered to hundreds of owning railroads, from pokey little shortlines to behemoth carriers like the mighty Pennsylvania Railroad which had nearly 3,000 "cabins," as cabooses were known on the PRR.

From the Depression to the 1980s, the decline of the caboose species was more or less gradual. But as the 1980s unfolded, the combination of new labor laws and advancing train-operation technology doomed the caboose almost overnight. By the start of the 1990s, the caboose had withered from an institution to that which today is largely a memory.

The kids in the back seat of dad's 1957 Mercury are probably delighted at being stopped by a passing freight of the Indiana Harbor Belt near Blue Island, Illinois, in July 1958. The caboose and its conductor are almost as much fun to watch for as the locomotives. *Richard J. Solomon*

CHAPTER ONE

THE CABOOSE
AND
ITS EVOLUTION

W hat did the little Auburn & Syracuse, a 26-mile railroad born in the early 1800s to connect its namesake cities in upstate New York, have to do with the caboose? By the end of the 1850s the line was gone, rendered into obscurity by being merged into the New York Central. Today most railroad historians wouldn't even remember the A&S. And yet, if the history books are correct, an icon of American railroading emerged from this fledgling carrier: the caboose.

Trains of the early nineteenth century were often but a rambling collection of both freight- and passenger-carrying cars—"mixed" trains. The

The red Santa Fe caboose in this 1975 scene on California's Cajon Pass is essentially the same as its ancestors from the turn of the century: a boxlike car-body—nearly identical in size to its ancestors—with an offset cupola riding and on two four-wheel trucks. The principal difference is that this caboose is of all-steel construction while earlier ones were wood. Contrast this to the Union Pacific diesel passing on the right: This 6,000-horsepower Electro-Motive (General Motors) behemoth represented state-of-the-art locomotive technology of the late 1960s and early 1970s—a vast change from locomotive technologies of two decades earlier, when steam still ruled the rails. Cabooses were indeed a stalwart icon of American railroading. The overall design of cabooses never really changed in their 150-year history. *Dan Pope collection*

9

Although probably constructed during the World War I era, this Great Northern wood caboose illustrates that caboose technology had not changed drastically from the formative years of American railroading of the previous century when most cabooses were but boxes on wheels. GN X715, shown in a fresh coat of paint at Superior, Wisconsin, in 1966, is still your basic box on wheels, although it does exhibit one important design change from cabooses of the mid-1800s in that the doors have been moved to the car ends. *Leon Onofri*

conductor, whose main duty was to supervise a train's operation as well as the transportation of travelers, had to improvise "office" space in which to do his paperwork. Sometimes it was in an empty set of passenger seats; other times it might have been in the corner of a baggage car.

In the 1840s, as the story goes, Auburn & Syracuse conductor Nat Williams had a better idea. He commandeered an empty box car, attached it to the mixed train of which he was in charge, and set up office. Seated on a box, he did his paperwork on a barrel, which also served as the dinner table when he drew victuals from the lunch pail he brought from home. He used the rest of the boxcar as a store room for lanterns, flags, tools, and spare car parts. The boxcar had become the "conductor's car."

As the popularity of rail transportation boomed in the mid-nineteenth century, the need

for separate freight and passenger trains became critical. On passenger-only trains, the conductor simply set up shop in the corner of one of the passenger cars, which is why passenger trains seldom carried cabooses despite the common public perception that they did. But, on a train that was made up entirely of freight cars, it was another story. Sure, the conductor could have shared space with the engine crew—which is what they do now—but back in the steam era, spacious locomotive cabs were a rare commodity. There was barely enough room for the engineer, his fireman, and a brakeman let alone the conductor and his desk.

On a freight train especially, the conductor needed his own car, particularly now that trains were getting longer. And here is where Nat Williams' idea of a conductor's car really began to catch on. Further, by placing this conductor's

The trainman riding the platform of Rio Grande Southern caboose 0400 assigned to a work train appears to be more cowhand than conductor. RGS was one of a litany of narrow-gauge railways built in Colorado during the state's silver era of the late nineteenth century, and very little had changed when this scene at Coke Ovens, Colorado, was recorded early in the 1950s. *Donald Robinson, Robert Willoughby Jones collection via Leon Onofri*

car at the end of the train, crews could better monitor the back half of a long freight, and the car could also serve as another brakeman's station. In those days before the invention of the automatic air-brake system, stopping a train meant dispatching the brakemen to race along the car roofs to activate each car's brakes. If you could do this from both ends of a train, with one brakeman stationed with the engine crew and one with the conductor in the conductor's car, then you stood a better chance of bringing the train to a timely halt.

"Conductor's car" was quite a mouthful, so somewhere along the line—and historical records are hazy, at best, on this—the word "caboose" came into common use in identifying the train's rolling office and storeroom. (Of course, over the years many other words—some not so complimentary—came to be used interchangeably with "caboose"; more about that elsewhere.) Reportedly, the word caboose was derived from the Dutch word *kabuis* and/or the German word *kabu-us*, both referring to the "little room" or galley where cooking was done on eighteenth century

11

Newark Public Library
Newark, New York 14513

As cupolas caught on in the late 1800s, some railroads employed the concept simply by adding cupolas to existing flattop cabooses. This Naumkeg Shortline caboose appears to have been a regular flattop car to which a somewhat crude, narrow, confining cupola was added. *Leon Onofri*

merchant ships. If this is so, then—and this is purely this writer's speculation—perhaps the term was first applied by Dutch men involved in early railroad activity. The Dutch were prominent early settlers in both the city and state of New York—territory that would later be served by lines of the New York Central System—so it is entirely possible that "caboose" was first used by Dutch railroaders on those lines.

Caboose Construction

Most American railroads were notoriously frugal, and though the concept of recycling is sometimes hailed with great fanfare in late twentieth century-America, it was hardly new to railroad companies even a hundred years earlier. Early cabooses were simple affairs that the railroads themselves

Erie caboose 04957 is a classic wooden cupola caboose from railroading's golden age, and painted bright red just as cabooses should be. Note the sheet-metal "awnings" over the windows. The caboose is shown on a switch job at Dayton, Ohio, in March 1955. *Cliff Comer, David P. Oroszi collection*

Because of the stresses cabooses endured in the line of duty, steel center-sills and underframes and, later, all-steel construction became paramount. Illustrating the need for steel-underframe cabooses is this scene of an east-bound Toledo, Peoria & Western freight being assisted up the hill out of East Peoria, Illinois, in May 1980 by visiting excursion steam locomotive Nickel Plate 765. Diesels are at the head end of the train (out of the photo) while the steam locomotive shoves against the rear end to the crest of the hill. In early days, many an all-wooden caboose was reduced to kindling by an overzealous engineer on the pusher locomotive. *Mike Schafer*

concocted, sometimes by simply modifying a boxcar that had seen better days. A more ambitious approach might be to hastily construct a shanty and plop it on a surplus flatcar. But either way, the conductor now had his own space. As trains grew longer, he would end up sharing it with a brakeman and a flagman.

Undoubtedly the most distinctive feature of a classic caboose is the cupola, that lofty perch from which the conductor and his brakeman could maintain vigil on the jostling collection of cars separating the caboose from the locomotive(s). At least one source credits the invention of

13

A Quick Lesson About Train Crews

Assuming you've read every word in this book so far, you've learned, if you already didn't know, that the conductor is the boss of the train. He tells the engineer when it's O.K. to depart from scheduled stops, and he keeps track of the train's business, checking freight waybills, "wheel reports," and switchlists as well as train orders from the dispatcher governing the specifics of the train's operation. And certainly nearly everyone knows what the engineer does: he or she operates the locomotive and its train. But what about the brakeman? Did they really have a separate person around to operate a train's brakes? Well, yes; long ago they did.

Prior to George Westinghouse's invention of the automatic air-brake system in 1869, trains had a rather haphazard and extraordinarily dangerous way of stopping. A locomotive had its own set of

With his brakeman about to climb aboard, the conductor of an eastbound Maine Central freight prepares to "highball" the yard at Brunswick, Maine, in October 1975. For a train's conductor and brakeman/flagman, the caboose was their rolling office and homestead. *Mike Schafer*

brakes while each car had its own manual brake, operated by turning a brake wheel atop the car. Whenever it was necessary to stop the train, the engineer applied the locomotive brakes and whistled for the brakemen to set the car brakes. This was accomplished by the hopefully agile brakemen clambering onto the car roofs and twisting the iron brake wheel to apply the car's brakes. Moving along the roof, the brakemen hopped from car to car—and keep in mind this had to be done in all kinds of weather while the train bounced and rocked along—repeating the procedure until enough brakes had been applied to bring the train to a halt. If all went well, this happened at the proper predetermined stopping location or, in the case of an emergency stop, well before contact with whatever was blocking the tracks (e.g., cows, stranded hay wagons, washed out bridges, and other trains). OSHA would not have been amused.

For the most part, the automatic air-brake system eliminated the dangers that beset brakemen. Now, not only did the engineer have control of the locomotive brakes, but he had at his immediate disposal a brake valve that activated every brake on every car in the train and yet another valve that operated both the locomotive's and train's brakes together. The brakeman's functions were now reduced to helping couple and uncouple cars, throwing switches, and, using flares, flags, or lanterns, protecting a stopped train from other nearby trains. To this day, all railroad cars still have manual brakes, activated by turning a big steel brake wheel, but they are no more than glorified parking brakes used for securing a car that has been isolated from the train. So, by the end of the nineteenth century, brakemen were no longer brakemen as such, but to this day the name refers to the person who assists in switching operations.

Until fairly recently it was common for a train crew to have two brakemen: a front or "head-end" brakeman and a rear brakeman. The head-end brakeman would assist the engineer in switching and train protection at the front of the train and rode in the locomotive while the rear brakeman, who shared caboose quarters with the conductor, helped with switching. In earlier days a flagman was assigned to protect either end of a stopped train by walking a predetermined distance from the end of the train to plant flares to warn approaching trains of a stopped train.

As a train moved over the railroad, crews went off duty at each division point and were replaced with a fresh or "rested" crew. Until American railroading began its drastic restructuring and modernization in the 1980s, division points were located about every 100-150 miles, an arbitrary distance that harkened to earlier times when it could indeed take 8-10 hours for a train to move that distance. On a Chicago-to-Los Angeles run, for example, a train might go through 15 crew changes. Crews were paid a day's wages to move a train over the division.

the cupola to T. B. Watson, a conductor on the Chicago & North Western in the 1860s.

It may well be an apocryphal story, but it sounds plausible: During one run across Iowa in 1863, conductor Watson was assigned to one of those crude, early cabooses—one that happened to have a person-size hole in the roof. During the journey, Watson perched himself on a stack of boxes such that he could protrude partway through the hole. And there he sat during the trip, enthralled by the 360-degree vista and of being able to see forward along the car roofs all the way to the locomotive. As the story goes, he convinced railroad shop forces to open up part of the roof of an existing (single-level) caboose and add an enclosed observation post, with windows all around. Thus was born the cupola. Now crews could maintain a far more thorough monitoring of their train. If this is all true, then the visionary Watson forever elevated the caboose to cult status, for it is the cupola that makes the traditional caboose one of the most distinctive pieces of railroad rolling stock.

The popularity of the cupola became widespread, although it appears this did not happen quickly. Not until the 1880s did references to cupolas—or "lookouts," as they were often known into the 1900s—become commonplace. Some railroads even took a step backward with the cupola design, opting to outfit the roof of a flattop caboose with a set of bench seats—open-air style. Although this incredibly thrifty approach to employing the cupola concept did indeed provide crews with all the advantages of a rooftop lookout, it did so at great cost to crew comfort and safety. Would you want to be the highest thing on a train rolling through a lightning storm?

Enhancing the cupola's distinction are the "porches"—platforms, if you will—that began appearing at either end of the caboose. This addition was a natural follow-up to the moving of caboose doors from the sides of the cars to the ends. End doors and platforms were considerably safer to deal with and greatly facilitated crews having to mount or dismount a caboose, which they often did while the train was still in (slow) motion. The platforms also provided yet another vantage point from which to monitor train operations. For example, a brakeman could stand on the rear platform to acknowledge any signals passed on by station agents and tower operators checking a passing train for defects such as sticking brakes, "hotboxes" (overheated wheel journals), or dragging equipment.

Early railroads often built all their own rolling stock, but as the need for passenger cars, boxcars, hoppers, flatcars, gondolas, cabooses, and other car types began to outstrip the ability of many of these railroads to keep up with the demands of outfitting their rapidly expanding physical plant, railcar-building enterprises began to sprout throughout the country. Many of these companies were but flash-in-the-pan endeavors whose names have long been forgotten or sentenced to obscurity. At best, however, some were absorbed by larger, more successful companies, firms like American Car & Foundry, St. Louis Car Company, Magor Car Corporation, Pullman-Standard Car Manufacturing Co., National Steel Car Corporation, and others. A few continue to build railcars today, though they probably haven't built any cabooses since the early 1980s.

As the need for cabooses became paramount for train operation, it was only natural that these car builders offered cabooses in their catalogs right along with a growing variety of boxcars, gondolas, and such. Nonetheless, a number of larger railroads which boasted complete car and locomotive shops continued to design and construct their own cabooses along with freight and passenger cars and even locomotives.

During the early twentieth century, with a new plenitude of car builders and railroad shops which could create railcars from raw materials, caboose building became almost an art unto itself. Primitive cabooses yielded to higher technology, better amenities, and more-specialized design. Carbuilding firms developed their own distinctive caboose styles despite having to work within parameters set forth by emerging national standards.

15

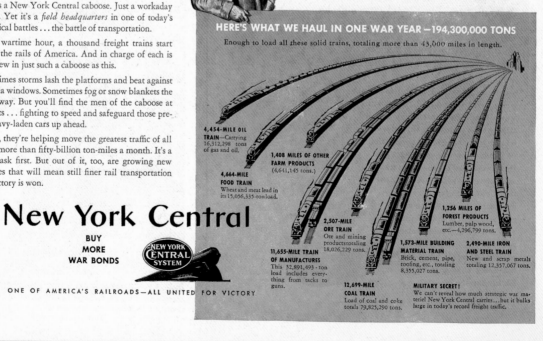

"RUNNING BOARD" IS TRAIN-TOP WALK

THE CONDUCTOR IS IN COMMAND
The Conductor has full charge of train operation. Here he is making up his "Wheel Report" showing the origin, destination and content of each car in his train.

NYC 19340

LOCKERS FOR CLOTHES, SUPPLIES

ICE BOX

Last but not Least...
the CABOOSE

OBSERVATION POST
From this seat in the caboose cupola, a brakeman keeps watch over the train ahead.

Command Car of a Mile-Long War Freight Train Rolling over the Water Level Route

RAILROAD WIGWAG
At stations and towers, and on passing trains, the men on duty watch each train, and signal to the train crew if anything needs attention. The rear brakeman receives and acknowledges these signals. A raised arm, like this, means, "All okay."

THIS is a New York Central caboose. Just a workaday little car. Yet it's a *field headquarters* in one of today's most critical battles...the battle of transportation.

Every wartime hour, a thousand freight trains start out over the rails of America. And in charge of each is a train crew in just such a caboose as this.

Sometimes storms lash the platforms and beat against the cupola windows. Sometimes fog or snow blankets the right of way. But you'll find the men of the caboose at their posts...fighting to speed and safeguard those precious, heavy-laden cars up ahead.

Today, they're helping move the greatest traffic of all time...more than fifty-billion ton-miles a month. It's a Victory task first. But out of it, too, are growing new efficiencies that will mean still finer rail transportation when Victory is won.

New York Central

BUY MORE WAR BONDS

NEW YORK CENTRAL SYSTEM

ONE OF AMERICA'S RAILROADS—ALL UNITED FOR VICTORY

HERE'S WHAT WE HAUL IN ONE WAR YEAR—194,300,000 TONS
Enough to load all these solid trains, totaling more than 43,000 miles in length.

4,454-MILE OIL TRAIN—Carrying 16,312,298 tons of gas and oil.

1,408 MILES OF OTHER FARM PRODUCTS (4,641,145 tons.)

4,664-MILE FOOD TRAIN Wheat and meat lead in its 15,056,335-ton load.

2,507-MILE ORE TRAIN Ore and mining products totaling 18,026,229 tons.

1,256 MILES OF FOREST PRODUCTS Lumber, pulp wood, etc.—4,296,799 tons.

11,655-MILE TRAIN OF MANUFACTURES This 32,891,493-ton load includes everything from tacks to guns.

1,573-MILE BUILDING MATERIAL TRAIN Brick, cement, pipe, roofing, etc., totaling 8,355,027 tons.

2,490-MILE IRON AND STEEL TRAIN New and scrap metals totaling 12,357,067 tons.

12,699-MILE COAL TRAIN Load of coal and coke totals 79,825,290 tons.

MILITARY SECRET! We can't reveal how much strategic war materiel New York Central carries...but it bulks large in today's record freight traffic.

The anatomy of a caboose. This World War II-era magazine ad from the New York Central—then one of the nation's leading railroads—showed that railroads back then had a knack for connecting to the public. NYC used the wartime analogy "field headquarters" in the "battle of transportation" to describe the function of cabooses, while the wonderful cutaway artwork revealed the inner workings of a typical crummy. Patriotic ad copy went on to say, "Every wartime hour, a thousand freight trains start out over the rails of America. And in charge of each is a train crew in just such a caboose as this." In the space of a day during the war, some 24,000 cabooses were rolling on U.S. rails. *Mike Schafer collection*

These involved dimensions for such things as car width, coupler and floor height (above railheads), and the need to be able to accommodate standardized car components such as brake rigging and air tanks. Some railroads which built their own cabooses, or at least had outside builders construct them to the railroad's own unique specifications, created cars so distinctive that they could only be associated with that railroad.

Eventually cabooses came equipped with all the comforts of home: beds, built-in desks, storage cabinets, stove, ice box, toilet, and some sort of lighting.

Many railroads upgraded their wooden cabooses by remounting their carbodies onto steel underframes. The steel underframe on which this wood-carbody Magma Arizona caboose sits is readily visible. *K. C. Henkels, Leon Onofri collection*

The Steel-Car Era

The emergence of steel—pound for pound stronger, lighter, and more tensile than iron (from which steel is refined)—in the mid-nineteenth century revolutionized manufacturing and construction worldwide. The first successful use of steel in the U.S. as a main structural component was in the Eads Bridge, opened in 1874 as the first road and railroad span across the Mississippi River at St. Louis. Despite the success of Eads (the bridge still stands and still carries road and rail traffic), it wouldn't be until the 1890s before steel replaced iron on a widespread basis in American manufacturing and industry.

The advent of steel was tremendously important to railroads. Locomotives and rolling stock—including cabooses—could be made larger and stronger; likewise, resilient steel (versus brittle iron) rails could carry far more weight and do it with greater safety while allowing faster speeds.

Save for wheel assemblies (trucks), early car construction was nearly entirely of wood—center-sills, underframes, and all. Iron underframes replaced wood, and then steel replaced iron. Car center-sills bear most of the brutal stresses of train movement, stresses which are transferred from car to car through the coupling system, which is integral to the center-sill. Such stresses not only result from cars being pulled along, but also when they are being shoved against one another either by a locomotive pushing against the train or by another phenomenon that occurs when cars bunch up against each other or snap apart from each other when brakes are applied or the train is rolling in uneven terrain—"slack action."

Steel and wood cabooses co-mingle on the Pennsylvania Railroad as one of PRR's hefty 2-10-0 locomotives shuffles them about the yard at Columbus, Ohio. On the PRR, cabooses were known as "cabins." The two steel cabins sandwiching the wood car in this scene are equipped with rooftop antennas for radio service. These were classed on the PRR as N-5c cabooses; unique were their porthole windows. *John Dziobko*

Steel center-sills and underframes were a solid advancement in car design, be it freight, passenger, or caboose. The toughness and flexibility of steel made it the perfect structural component for car underframes. Since most stresses are absorbed by the center-sill, railroads and car builders were free to continue using wood—cheap, versatile, and readily available—for most of the rest of a car's construction, mainly the car sides, roof, and flooring. Construction of wood-body, steel-underframe cars continued well into the twentieth century.

As steel production became more widespread and competitive, it also became less expensive, and railroads began using more of it in car construction. Despite all the advantages of wood mentioned above, wood-body cars had a serious drawback: In the event of an accident, they could instantly be transformed into a pile of kindling. Further, wood burns very nicely, thank you, and fire was the bane of wood freight cars in general and cabooses in particular. Cabooses had to be heated and lighted, and in earlier days this was accomplished with coal stoves and kerosene lamps—both of which were also adept at accomplishing spectacular conflagrations. Too, wooden cars rotted easily if not constantly maintained with periodic trips to the shops to replace damaged wood and be repainted.

Following World War I, all-steel car construction accelerated, and by the Depression a majority of newly constructed freight cars and cabooses were of all-steel design, which provided maximum strength and safety albeit at some expense in terms of weight. Meanwhile, wood carbody rolling stock was often upgraded by being sheathed in sheet steel for added strength and fire resistance.

That's not to say wood cars disappeared during that period. Indeed, wood-body freight cars and cabooses in particular survived in active service well into the 1970s, when laws governing interstate commerce began restricting the interchange of wood-body cars between railroads. (Around World War I, and for obvious safety reasons, the construction of wood-body passenger cars had ceased although a number of wood passenger cars

All-steel construction of passenger cars, freight cars, and cabooses gained momentum after World War I. Industry giant Santa Fe purchased its first all-steel cabooses in 1927. By 1950 Santa Fe rostered 901 steel cabooses, 501 built by American Car & Foundry and 400 built by the railroad's own shops. All of the cars were overall similar in appearance to the wooden cabooses they superseded. In this photo taken at Joliet, Illinois, in 1978, one of those all-steel cabooses enjoys a "second life" after having been upgraded by the railroad in the late 1960s with cushioned underframe, refurbished crew quarters, sealed windows, and a bright red-and-yellow paint scheme. Look closely to see where some of the original windows had been blanked over. *Steve Smedley*

Another popular option for strengthening a wood-body caboose, particularly those built with steel underframes to begin with, was to sheath the carbody in steel. This Soo Line caboose in Waukesha, Wisconsin, in 1967 has been partially sheathed in steel (note the seams on the car sides), and steel rods help to reinforce the wooden cupola. The yellow ends were a relatively new twist in a world still dominated by all-red cabooses. Yellow was a better reflectant of a locomotive headlight. *Thomas Hoffmann*

remained in service long after; eventually many were sheathed in steel.) This safety issue caught up with cabooses, and by World War II, all-steel construction became the norm for newly manufactured cabooses.

The Bay-Window Alternative

With the steel caboose came another development likened to that of the invention of the cupola: the bay-window. Although bay-window caboose design had little to do with steel construction per se (there were in fact wooden bay-window cabooses), its appearance and widening acceptance coincided with the all-steel car advancement. In the bay-window caboose, a portion of the wall with one set of windows on each side of the car was projected out from the main side wall to form a small alcove in which the brakeman and conductor, seated, could look forward at their train. The bay windows supplanted the need for a cupola.

Many railroads felt this design had several advantages over the cupola caboose. For Eastern railroads long plagued with clearance restrictions—particularly in tunnels—harkening to the earliest construction years of American railroads,

21

Chicago, Milwaukee, St. Paul & Pacific—The Milwaukee Road—is credited with masterminding the bay-window caboose. In 1939, the railroad began mass producing all-steel bay-window cabooses. More than 300 of them, such as the 01895 at Sparta, Wisconsin, in 1973, bore Milwaukee Road's trademark ribbed sides. The railroad used ribbing on many of its home built passenger cars, boxcars, and cabooses as a way of strengthening the car without adding too much weight. *Mike Schafer*

the bay-window caboose was a better fit. Too, as railroads modernized, freight cars got larger and taller, restricting the forward view that the cupola offered. Not that that mattered much. Most problems that occurred with a train happened along the sides of the cars or in the wheel areas, all of which were easier to eyeball from a bay window.

In addition, bay-window cars were cheaper and safer. The complexities of constructing a cupola and its associated structural members were eliminated, and without the high cupola ceiling, bay-window cabooses were easier to heat. The safety issue was another, increasingly important

matter. If a crew member is going to be caught off guard by slack action (see Chapter 3, Hazards of Caboose Life, on this topic), better that the crew person be at floor level than perched in a cupola—or worse, in the process of climbing into one. Ironically, although C&NW conductor T. B. Watson is credited with inspiring the cupola concept, that railroad was one of the first to discourage their use, some 100 years later.

Milwaukee Road and Baltimore & Ohio are often credited as pioneers in the introduction of bay-window caboose design. The Milwaukee experimented by building several bay-window cars

22

Baltimore & Ohio was another pioneer in the realm of bay-window cabooses. Like Milwaukee Road, many of the B&O cars had their own unique character stamp—in this case the "wagontop" roof, a design feature also found on B&O freight cars. B&O C-2405 is at Chicago in 1966. *Leon Onofri collection*

out of regular wooden cupola cabooses in 1937-38. The cupolas were removed, the roofs redone, and windowed bay alcoves grafted onto the sides. These "Frankenbooses" (this writer's term, not the railroad's) were deemed a success and served as the prototype for future cars.

In 1939, work began at the road's famous Milwaukee Shops—known for being able to build just about anything the railroad needed—for a whole series of all-steel "rib-side" bay-window cabooses to be produced in-house, production-line style. The ribbing feature was unique to the Milwaukee Road. Narrow steel ribs were welded to the car side panels for added strength

and to prevent the car from sagging. The railroad ended up doing seven production runs from 1939 through 1951, outshopping 315 "rib-siders."

The Best of Both Worlds

During the 1950s, another caboose innovation began to catch on that embraced the advantages of both the cupola and bay window. What became known as the "extended-vision cupola" (EVC) caboose basically was more of a refinement to cupola design rather than bay-window design. In it, the cupola was extended outward beyond the standard width of the car in what was sometimes known as a "saddlebag" design. Now crews could

WHAT'S IN A NAME?

Railroaders are legendary when it comes to coining nicknames for just about any aspect of their work, so it's no surprise that the caboose commanded a special place in the realm of railroad lingo. The most widely known "generic" nickname for a caboose? Undoubtedly "crummy." But other names aptly illustrate the terms of endearment crews had for cabooses, to one degree or another: hack, buggy, brain box, dog house, parlor, chariot, and—in reference to conductor the conductor being the boss of the train—throne room and clown wagon, to name just a few. Even the caboose cupola enjoyed its own nicknames, like "sun parlor," "dog house," and—among the earliest—the "lookout."

Beyond the endearment level, several railroads had their own—almost official—names for cabooses. On at least three lines, the Santa Fe; Chicago & North Western; and Chicago, Burlington & Quincy, cabooses were nearly always referred to as "way cars." The term is in reference to a time when many freight trains carried a car—often a boxcar but sometimes a caboose—assigned specifically to a scheduled train for purposes of handling LCL (less-than-carload) freight to small towns visited by the train. On the late, great Pennsylvania Railroad, cabooses were always referred to as "cabins" or "cabin cars." On the Boston & Maine they were "buggies," and on most Canadian railways, cabooses were "vans."

look along the sides of their trains as well as forward and above.

Again, the clearance restrictions that continued to hamper some Eastern railroads precluded the extended-vision cupola caboose from gaining wide acceptance east of Chicago, but elsewhere the concept caught on well. The Duluth, Missabe & Iron Range Railroad claims to have spawned the extended-vision idea, but Indiana's Monon Railroad (pronounced MOE-non) may have been the first to actually build a bay-window-cupola caboose, which it did at its shop complex in Lafayette, Indiana.

Regardless of who was first, the design came to be most closely associated with the International Car Corporation, headquartered in Buffalo, New York. International built thousands of EVC cabooses in the 1960s, 1970s, and early 1980s for dozens of railroads. Indeed, International became the largest producer of all types of cabooses in general.

The Comforts of Home

Quite literally, cabooses were homes on wheels, especially when crews were assigned to specific cars and used them as hostelries at the away-from-home end of a run. If you're going to live in a caboose, it had better be livable. Most were, to one degree or another. Bunks were provided for sleeping, chairs for sitting, closets for storing, sinks for washing, and toilets for . . . uh, reading.

Throughout most of caboose history, heating was traditionally accomplished through good old-fashioned coal-fired iron stoves—Estate being a common brand—which of course also doubled as cooking stoves. Wood stoves were not uncommon in areas of the country where trees were abundant, but since most trains until after World War II were powered by coal-fired steam locomotives, coal was also a natural for caboose heating. However, with the virtual disappearance of the steam locomotive during the 1950s came the coal stove's fall from grace. Since railroads no longer needed to maintain a reserve of coal for locomotives, then many certainly weren't going to maintain any for coal stoves, however minimal the

The all-welded steel cabooses of the Wabash Railroad and its one-time affiliate, the Ann Arbor Railroad, featured cupolas that had sloping sides and rounded corners, giving the cars a modernistic flare. One of the distinctive cars stands at Elberta (Frankfort), Michigan, as an Ann Arbor diesel pauses in its switching duties on a December night in 1971. *Jim Heuer*

requirements. Oil-fired stoves gained favor. Aside from being easier to ignite and maintain, they were cleaner and safer.

Caboose lighting followed a similar evolution. Early interior lighting was provided by oil or kerosene chimney or "caboose" lamps. Exterior lights, specifically the two red-and-green "marker" lamps mounted on the back of a caboose of a "live" train, were also kerosene or oil. (Caboose and marker lamps alike are today highly sought-after antiques.) The inherent danger of easily toppled oil or kerosene lamps is obvious, yet electric lighting wasn't quite as quick to catch on in the caboose as it was in the average American home. Cabooses always had to carry their own source of power for lighting, and oil was more convenient than having to install and maintain some sort of electric generator. But it was only a matter of time. Eventually cabooses came equipped with (or older cabooses upgraded with) alternator-generators driven by belts linked to wheel axles. Now all car lighting inside and out (as well as hot plates for cooking) could be electrified. When the car was not in motion, storage batteries kept the electrons flowing.

Just as there was a need for heating and lighting, there was also a need for refrigeration, especially on cabooses that served as ersatz homes in over-the-road service. Since crews sometimes lived in cabooses for longer periods than they did at home, the need for food storage was paramount. As in real homes, early caboose refrigerators were in fact "ice boxes"—insulated boxes, usually metal, with a compartment for a block of

Monon Railroad was one of the first—if not *the* first—to employ the "extended-vision cupola" design, shown on this caboose trailing a northbound freight near Westville, Indiana, in December 1971. In the 1950s, Monon took several of its standard steel cupola cabooses and added bay windows on either side of their cupolas. Car manufacturers followed suit, but with a slightly different approach to the design, instead incorporating a wide "saddlebag" cupola rather than a cupola with bay windows. *Jim Heuer*

26

The extended-vision caboose proved popular on many railroads during the 1970s and 1980s. Graphically illustrating the difference between extended-vision cupola and bay-window cabooses is this view on the St. Louis-San Francisco (Frisco) Railway freight at Cuba, Missouri, in 1980. The westbound freight has one of each trailing. *Mike Schafer*

ice which cooled adjacent compartments. Home refrigeration went electric mostly after the Depression, but cabooses continued to employ ice-cooled refrigerators well into the 1960s—long after axle-generated electricity had gained wide acceptance for caboose lighting. By the end of the 1960s, electric refrigeration finally caught on, for water coolers as well as caboose refrigerators.

Although belt- or shaft-driven (off one of the caboose's axles) alternator-generators triumphed as the tried and true method of producing electricity on most cabooses that were electrified, a few railroads boldly tinkered with alternate methods. Milwaukee Road experimented with roof-mounted propane-powered thermal-electrical generators; the propane was stored in tanks mounted beneath the caboose floor. Unfortunately, propane tanks were awkward to recharge, and anything mounted on the roof of a caboose was severely subject to the elements, thus dooming that experiment. At least one railroad, North Carolina's Durham & Southern, tried propeller-driven generators. Also roof-mounted, they were plagued with the same problem as Milwaukee's thermal generators. Too, propeller generators relied heavily on continuous train movement. As any freight train crew will tell you, freight trains can be particularly adept at standing still.

One quite successful alternate method of producing electricity for cabooses was the use of a diesel-powered generator. Although this approach necessitated some sort of fuel storage tank on the caboose, a diesel power plant provided a strong, ongoing source of electricity whether or not the caboose was moving—as long as there was fuel, of course.

For about as long as cabooses (and railroad passenger cars, for that matter) existed, railroads employed in them an extremely practical form of toilet plumbing design, the "dry" hopper. Some might call it "straight-to-the-tracks" plumbing, returning to Mother Earth that which Mother Earth had, more or less, produced in the first place. Eventually, however, many would come to call it "politically incorrect" plumbing, the direct result of which was introduction of the retention toilet on some cabooses. The State of Washington, which had special environmental concerns, was a pioneer in such matters, and state law required that all cabooses operating in or through Washington state be equipped with retention toilets. By the 1970s, the federal government was heavily involved in railroad safety regulations and related improvements, and retention toilets were high on the list of these changes.

Air-conditioning was a modern miracle virtually lost upon the caboose, even though it was widely being applied to railroad passenger cars beginning around the time of World War I. Nearly all early cabooses had "armstrong" air-conditioning, though; i.e., push on the window until it slides open. Any moving caboose equipped with window screens would stay reasonably comfortable in all but the most sultry weather conditions. Railroad conductors can probably thank vandals more than anyone for accelerating the acceptance of true air-conditioning. As more windows were violated by stone (or gun) wielding punks, federal regulations began requiring railroads to install (unopenable) windows made of bulletproof Plexiglas. Now the only way to sufficiently cool a caboose was to install an electro-mechanical air-conditioning system.

Communications and the Caboose

Until after World War II, communication between locomotive and caboose crews—sometimes separated by more than a mile of train—was accomplished largely through whistle signals from the locomotive crew. Through a combination of short and/or long blasts of the whistle, the engineer could, for example, signal the caboose crew that the train was about to stop and that the flagman would need to protect the rear of the train. Caboose crew members, while on the ground near their stopped train, could provide the head-end crew with certain basic instructions—proceed, back up, and so forth—through hand lantern signals (the same could also be accomplished with lighted flares). For example, a vertical swing of the lantern or flare signaled the engineer to "highball"—that is, proceed ahead.

Radio was the ideal replacement to such cumbersome methods of communication, and in 1947 radios were first installed on cabooses, allowing direct contact between locomotive and caboose crews. Today, two-way radios are compact devices easily carried in coat pockets, but in those days radio equipment involved complex circuitry, hefty antennas, bulky vacuum tubes, and furniture-size batteries. Much of this equipment was hung from the ceilings and mounted under seating or bunks. Naturally, radio communication caught on in a big way, and by the end of the 1950s any truly modern railroad worth its salt had "radio equipped" emblazoned on the sides of its cabooses (and

Electric power was late in coming to the world of cabooses, where heating and lighting were long in the domain of fuel oil. This upgraded Southern Pacific bay-window caboose, shown in Klamath Falls, Oregon, in 1982, features electric power. Note the blue, belt-driven generator-alternator assembly mounted on the car's lead truck. *Jim Mischke*

sometimes locomotives). Whether or not the trackside uninformed fully understood the meaning of this was beside the point. ("Boy, life in the caboose must be good if you can tune in Jack Benny while you're working!")

As radio technology became more refined, the radio-equipped caboose actually became an anachronism. No longer was radio equipment considered an appliance to be installed; now radios were portable and could be assigned to crews rather than to cabooses.

The Final Modern Era of the Caboose

The more things change, the more they stay the same, you know. That time-worn adage fits the caboose. Stand back and look at some of the final cabooses manufactured in the late 1970s and early 1980s—yes, there are a few cabooses still around—and compare them to crummies from a half century earlier. Outwardly anyway, the overall design is still a box on wheels with a cupola or bay window. Save for the extended-vision cupola, most of the evolution from World War II forward has been internal, from electric generation to radio communication and other items we've cussed and discussed.

Likewise, the final refinements to the caboose prior to its rather sudden demise in the 1980s and 1990s were also largely internal. These included things like better wall insulation, aluminum roofs, and all-welded construction, but most notable was the development of the cushioned underframe—the final attempt at addressing the age-old problem (as old as cabooses themselves) of slack action.

The cushion-underframe concept, first applied to freight cars, involves a draft gear—that's the whole coupler assembly—which is attached to the underframe through a sprung arrangement that absorbs the shock of one car suddenly being pulled or thrust against an adjacent car. The cushioned underframe thus became not only a wonder drug for alleviating damage to freight, but for lessening—on cabooses—damage to conductor/brakeman/flagman arms, legs, vertebras, and craniums.

In a like manner, other late-era improvements focused on safety. Interior fixtures and appliances were designed with rounded corners to reduce injuries, while more and more caboose platforms were being constructed of safety tread steelwork for more-positive footing. Seating now consisted of foam-filled cushions for added comfort and safety, and high backs reduced whiplash injuries resulting from slack action. As in the automobile, seatbelts became a not-uncommon fixture in cupolas.

All the refinements and developments that the caboose enjoyed over its century and a half history took their toll: In the long run they resulted in the caboose being an expensive proposition to buy and maintain; making cabooses an easy target for cost-saving hawks in railroad management. Now looming on the horizon was the ultimate "refinement" of the caboose: its replacement by an electronic end-of-train (EOT) device. We'll save that sad story for a later chapter.

The interior of a modern Canadian National caboose shows recessed steps to the cupola seating area, safety-tread cupola flooring, wide rear window with rear-facing chair, high-back seats, and grab-irons on the ceiling as an aid to walking in a moving car. The car's manual brake wheel is visible outside the door. *Don Jilson*

CHAPTER TWO

CABOOSES, THEIR TYPES AND USES

Not all trains are alike. Oh, freight trains may all look alike to the average bystander, but—operationally, at least—they can differ in many ways. You have long-distance runs, local trains that stop to work lineside industries, transfer jobs between yards in major cities, and a host of specialized movements such as work trains.

Likewise, not all locomotives are created equal. There are fast passenger locomotives, high-horsepower freight locomotives for over-the-road work, and switching locomotives for shifting cars in a yard. It stands to reason, then, that not all cabooses are or were alike either. Indeed, there

The grimy bay-window caboose of a passing Erie Lackawanna freight contrasts with the brightly colored rows of brand-new cabooses parked outside the International Car Company plant at Kenton, Ohio, in August 1975. Out of the dozens of carbuilders that have served American railroads since the nineteenth century, International rose to be leader in caboose construction. *Mike Schafer*

The first cabooses were not much more than boxes on wheels, but this no-frills design survived the ages. In modern-day railroading, box-style cabooses worked fine for local-type service. Missouri Pacific caboose 11960 is one of those creatures—no cupola, no bay window; in fact, hardly any windows at all. It rests for the night with an MP diesel at St. Genevieve, Missouri, in October 1980. Note the "FOR YARD AND TRANSFER SERVICE ONLY" stenciled on the side of the caboose. *Mike Schafer/Garland McKee*

Clad in dark red, the pair of cabooses bobbing along at the end of a Buffalo-bound Wabash freight at Windsor, Ontario, in 1960 epitomize the classic wooden cupola caboose of the early twentieth century. Officially concluding the train are two oil-fired marker lamps hung on the rear of the trailing caboose. The marker lamps were hung by the caboose crew at the start of a trip. *Dave Ingles*

was a dizzying array of caboose styles and types, each one tailored to different needs and job functions, whether the car was manufactured by a car builder or a railroad. What follows is a non-scientific overview of the many different inhabitants of the caboose kingdom.

Box-On-Wheels Flattop Caboose

The earliest cabooses were not much more than boxes on wheels, and in fact, many early cabooses were simply converted boxcars. There was no cupola, and even bay windows were still nearly a century away. These early cars usually had side (versus end) doors, maybe a few windows, and rudimentary interiors.

From these ancient cars evolved all manner of cabooses—cupola, bay-window, transfer, drover, and more. Yet, even in modern times there was still a call for the primordial box-on-wheels caboose. Some railroads felt that a no-frills caboose was perfectly adequate for very short runs such as transfer movements between yards in a big city. Such low-speed movements did not require a crew to keep a constant vigil on the train, so cupolas and bay windows really weren't necessary. Also, the fact that crews assigned to such jobs usually didn't spend as much time in the caboose was reflected by the car's interior amenities—or lack of them.

Such cabooses were cheap to acquire or build. They made ideal fill-in time projects for railroad

35

Newark Public Library
Newark, New York 14513

Small in stature, but big in terms of historical significance, bobber No. 10 of the Delaware & Hudson Canal Company enjoys its own custom-made shelter at a park in Oneonta, New York. In this little red caboose on September 13, 1883, the mighty Brotherhood of Railroad Trainmen was born. *C. W. Newton*

shop forces, and if they could be built from old boxcars or troop sleepers left over from World War II, so much the better. Despite the minimalistic nature of this early "design," such as it was, it found a niche in modern-day railroading.

Bobbers

Early cabooses that were built new—versus cobbled out of old boxcars and such—often were small and rode on four rigid-mounted wheels rather than the more-common arrangement of two four-wheel swivel truck assemblies. These cars acquired the nicknames of "bobbers" and "bouncers"—probably because of the ride quality delivered by a rigid wheelbase.

Their Lilliputian stature and rideability eventually rendered bobbers largely to the "curiosities" section of railroad history books. The railroad

Norfolk & Western was one of numerous Eastern railroads favoring bay-window cabooses, and, at least in this scene at N&W's huge yard in Portsmouth, Ohio, bay-window cars outnumber cupola cars four to one. Note the small upper bunk windows directly above the regular side windows. This unusual feature was found on bay-window cabooses of the Nickel Plate Road, which once owned these cars. Nickel Plate was merged into N&W in 1964. *David P. Oroszi*

Peoria & Eastern 21496 tagging behind the daily eastbound P&E freight at Le Roy, Illinois, in October 1975 represents a sort of "poor man's" bay-window car. Unlike regular bay-window cabooses where the seating area was partially in the bay, only the side windows themselves in this car were bayed. Although cheaper to construct, this arrangement was not as convenient for crews, which had to lean into the window area to view fore and aft. *Mike Schafer*

boom of the mid-nineteenth century demanded larger locomotives and railcars, and larger cabooses necessitated more-traditional wheel arrangements. Nonetheless, one of the most famous cabooses in American history was a bobber.

On September 13, 1883, Delaware & Hudson Canal Co. caboose No. 10, parked in the D&H freight yards at Oneonta, New York, was the chosen location for a meeting of minds determined to form a union that could fight for better working conditions. The idea flew, and the Brotherhood of Railroad Brakemen—later renamed Brotherhood of Railroad Trainmen—was born. In 1924 the D&H put the caboose on display in a park in Oneonta where it remains to this day.

Cupola Cabooses

The cupola caboose hardly needs an introduction. It's the type of caboose against which all others are compared; it's the type of caboose

WHAT POSITION THE CUPOLA?

Once railroads had established that cupolas were a good thing, they had to determine just exactly where on the roof they worked best. Centered? Off center? Far end? There never really appeared to be a definitive conclusion—at least not on an industrywide basis, and not even on some individual railroads.

Off center: Most cupolas were offset from center, permitting better utilization of space on the deck floor for desks, bunks, and kitchen facilities.

Smack in the middle: Symmetry simplified design and construction. Forward visibility from cupola was the same regardless of the direction that the caboose faced.

All the way to the end: Relatively rare, placement to the extreme end allowed room for bunks, desks, and kitchen facilities in small cabooses; also allowed crews quick access between cupola and end platform.

Union Pacific steel cabooses had extra high cupolas positioned in the middle of the car. UP 25322 is at Laramie, Wyoming, in 1981. *Thomas Hoffmann*

LEFT
Off-center cupolas such as this on a freshly painted caboose of the Elgin, Joliet & Eastern in 1985, were once all the rage. *Mike Schafer*

RIGHT
The extreme: Delaware & Hudson 35849R at Greenwich Junction, New York, in 1977 has a cupola that's as far to one side as it can get without falling off the roof. *Scott Hartley*

Upgrading a caboose to include a bay window was relatively easy—at least easier than adding a cupola—and as the bay-window design caught on, several railroads modified existing cupola or box cabooses with bays. Such is what happened to this wooden Kewaunee, Green Bay & Western caboose. The bay section itself is steel. *K. C. Henkels, Leon Onofri collection*

(painted red, of course) most people think of when you say "caboose."

"Imagineered" in 1863 (see Chapter 1), the cupola gained widespread acceptance by the end of the nineteenth century by providing an ideal "crow's nest" from which train crews could maintain vigil on their rolling warehouse. Cupola cabooses—and cupolas themselves, for that matter—came in all shapes and sizes. Cupolas became fixtures on cabooses of all sorts, ranging from diminutive bobbers to International Car

Company's roomy extended-vision cabooses. Clearance restrictions—long the bane of many Northeastern railroads—dictated squat cupolas for some roads if they had them at all, while cabooses of some Midwestern and Western roads had cupolas of penthouse proportions. Even the positioning of a cupola varied. Offset from center was perhaps most common—and classic—but some caboose types, such as the "Northeastern" style shared by Reading Company, Western Maryland, Lehigh Valley, and other lines of the mid-Atlantic region,

Many traits of the New York Central System permeated successor Conrail, among them the preference for bay-window cabooses. Conrail even went so far as to close off the cupola and add bay windows to this former New Haven caboose, shown in Buffalo, New York, in 1976. *Thomas Hoffmann*

put them smack in the center of the car. A few put them at an extreme end, presumably for quick access to the end door nearest the cupola, but at the expense of aesthetics—such cabooses had a rather unbalanced appearance.

Largely for safety reasons, cupolas fell into disfavor on a few lines beginning in the 1950s. These railroads either purchased new cabooses sans cupolas or blocked off the cupola windows of existing cars . . . or both. Fortunately for those who cherish cupolaed cars, the cupola remained

popular on a number of railroads right up to the end of the caboose era.

Bay-Window Cabooses

Pioneered by Milwaukee Road and Baltimore & Ohio in the late 1930s, the bay-window caboose proved a worthy opponent to the cupola concept. The bay window eliminated the dangers associated with the cupola while permitting crews forward vision along the sides of the trains—where most problems lurked anyway. By the late 1930s, freight

41

THE "NORTHEASTERN" CABOOSE

In the mid-1930s, the Reading Railroad (pronounced RED-ding), of Monopoly© board-game fame, developed a design for a 32-foot, all-steel, center-cupola caboose which it began building in its own shops in Reading, Pennsylvania, in1936. Hallmark of the design were two sets of paired windows on each side and a centered cupola with sloped sides. The design was adopted by Reading's close ally, the Lehigh Valley Railroad, which applied it to more than 250 cabooses built at its shops in Sayre, Pennsylvania. One of the cabooses was even on display at the 1939 New York World's Fair.

Still other railroads acquired rights to the design, which became known as the "Northeastern" caboose style, and even New Haven (Connecticut)-based A. C. Gilbert, longtime manufacturer of American Flyer electric toy trains, produced models of the Northeastern caboose. Eventually, not only could Northeastern cabooses be found on Eastern roads like Western Maryland and Lehigh New England, but also on roads that purchased them secondhand: Chicago & North Western, Cedar Rapids & Iowa City, and Oregon's City of Prineville Railway.

Reading Company originated the "Northeastern"-style all-steel caboose. Still close to its as-built condition, one of the cabooses tags along with a switch engine working near Reading's passenger depot at Harrisburg, Pennsylvania, in 1965. *John Dziobko*

Chesapeake & Ohio 3296 trailing an eastbound freight at Wellsboro, Indiana, in the summer of 1986 illustrates what the "extended" in extended-vision cupola means. This is very much a classic EVC caboose of the International Car Company. *Mike Schafer*

cars were getting larger and taller, thus inhibiting the forward view provided by cupolas.

Bay-window cabooses were not subject to overhead clearance restrictions, and they were cheaper to build and easier to heat or air condition. Crews had quick access to the bay section from car ends and vice versa, not having to clamber up into the cupola section.

Most bay-window designs called for a full top-to-bottom bay area, allowing train crews to comfortably sit at their desks or seats in the bay section and look forward, but on a few railroads such as

43

Chicago Great Western caboose No. 10, resting at Sycamore, Illinois, in July 1965 as a switcher works nearby, was an ancient, wood-body cupola caboose that had been converted to an ersatz extended-vision car. The revised cupola appears to have been concocted through a combination of wood and sheet-metal components. *Terry Norton*

New York Central, only the window section was bayed. Though cheaper to build, the drawback of this design was that it required crew members to lean into the bay area to look forward or behind.

Extended-Vision Cupola Cabooses

Whereas the bay-window caboose design generally superseded the long-entrenched cupola design, the extended-vision cupola (EVC) or "saddlebag" caboose extolled the virtues of both the cupola and the bay window. In them, the cupolas borrowed the bay window design by protruding beyond the standard car width, thereby providing train crews with a lofty means of watching the top and the sides of their train.

Despite the growing popularity of the bay-window caboose, EVC cabooses enjoyed great popularity among numerous railroads in the postwar years right up through the end of the caboose era. Although the Monon and the Duluth, Missabe & Iron Range are credited with ushering in the saddlebag cupola concept, the design became a hallmark of the International Car Company, the leading manufacturer of American cabooses.

Transfer cabooses are commonly used in busy urban regions webbed by rail lines and yards. Such is the case in the Wilkes-Barre/Scranton area of eastern Pennsylvania, where in 1980 a Conrail transfer with a traditional platform transfer caboose creeps toward the next stop while another local putts overhead. This is a relatively new car, with safety-tread platforms. *Mike Schafer*

International's extended-vision model—sometimes referred to as the "Wide Vision Cupola Caboose"—were the Cadillacs of American cabooses, and many are still in use as this volume goes to press.

Work and Transfer Cabooses

Overshadowed by important through freights and intermodal (container and "piggyback" truck) trains, transfer runs and work trains required an entirely different type of caboose.

Transfer trains are generally found in large cities like Chicago, St. Louis, Kansas City, and Los Angeles where the numerous freight yards of the various railroads have a need to be interlinked. As an example, let's suppose that it's 1965 and a New York Central freight has arrived at Gibson Yard on Chicago's far southeast side. A number of the cars on the train, which originated in the East, are destined for points on the Chicago & North Western in Minnesota and Iowa. These are switched out and put on a transfer run of the Indiana Harbor Belt Railroad—a terminal railroad serving Chicago—and run up to C&NW's huge Proviso Yard on the western fringes of Chicago.

Transfer cabooses with extended end platforms are also ideal for work-train service. This Southern Pacific car—a rarity in that it wears the road's "Daylight" paint scheme, which saw only limited application after the 1950s—is being used on a water train in 1990. Crews are hosing down the right-of-way to reduce fire hazard and dust. *Brian Solomon*

This distance traveled by this transfer is only a little more than 30 miles, and it involves only a few hours—not the 12 or 14 hours that an over-the-division run might require. A transfer caboose (or "doghouse," as it is sometimes known) and its close cousin, the work caboose, need only provide the basics: shelter and a place to do paperwork. Beds are not necessary, and since most crews will simply pack a lunch from home, the need for stoves, sinks, refrigerators, and storage facilities is negligible. Cupolas and perhaps even bay windows are unnecessary, since transfer runs and

work trains are by nature plodding and therefore less prone to incidents of hotboxes and such.

The traditional transfer caboose design harkens to one of the earliest of caboose designs, that of a shanty on a flatcar. As such, this works well for transfer service. A modest-size cabin is sufficient for the conductor's desk, crew chairs, and small storage area while the ample platform areas outside provide a place to haul work material, extra car components, and tools. Another popular transfer-caboose style is the tried-and-proven "box on wheels"—no cupola or bay windows, only end doors and short platforms.

Indiana Harbor Belt 67 is a homemade transfer caboose, rebuilt from a standard cupola caboose acquired from the Santa Fe. In the rebuild process, the cupola was lopped off and most of the windows blanked out. The IHB is a terminal switching road serving the Chicago area. *Thomas Hoffmann*

The straightforward qualities of transfer and work cabooses made them ideal side projects for railroads which built their own rolling stock; they could be cobbled together using components from retired regular cabooses and freight cars. In some cases, this resulted in some pretty distinctive contraptions.

Specialty and Miscellaneous

There was probably a caboose made for just about every need, no matter how esoteric or specialized. Railcar manufacturers offered specialty cabooses, and railroads which boasted talented shop forces often either constructed their own from the ground up or customized cabooses that were already on hand. When railroads created their own specialty cabooses, there seemed to be few rules other than they had to fit the track gauge and be compatible with more-conventional equipment at least in terms of having standard couplers and braking systems.

One of the more widely recognized specialty types were the "drover" cabooses. Indigenous to Western railroads, drover cabooses were used on livestock trains to accommodate not only the train crew but cattlemen (drovers) accompanying the doomed steers, pigs, and sheep from the open ranges to stockyard centers such as Kansas City and Chicago. Drover cabooses were outfitted with extra seats and bunks for the extra "passengers" and by that necessity were usually longer than the typical caboose and had more windows.

A similar scenario was carried out on railroads throughout the country that handled regular,

continued on page 50

NEXT PAGES
Louisville & Nashville 6611 is a transfer-style caboose with a mainline twist in that it sports bay windows. It trails a unit-coal train near Lot, Kentucky, in May 1982. *David P. Oroszi*

This outside-braced work caboose on the Rock Island may have been rebuilt from an old wood boxcar. As a caboose, it features a cupola and side door for loading company materials and other incidental freight or supplies. When photographed at Maryland Heights, Missouri, near St. Louis, in 1975, the car was assigned to a switch job working an industrial park that required many back-up moves. *Paul Dalman*

Continued from page 47

ticket-bearing passengers in cabooses. Although this was a common practice early in the century, particularly on branch lines where business and population did not warrant full-scale passenger service, safety and space considerations (plus the fact that everyone in the U.S. would eventually come to own their own Chevy, Ford, or Toyota) gradually led railroads to end this type of passenger accommodation. Nonetheless, as late as the 1980s one could purchase a ticket and legally ride a caboose on certain trains of the Georgia Railroad, the Tucson, Cornelia & Gila Bend, and the Soo Line, although by this time the Soo would accommodate only one passenger at a

time. The road's newer cabooses only had one spare seat, and safety regulations stated that any passengers had to be seated when the train was starting or stopping.

Railroads sometimes customized cabooses of otherwise traditional design. Illinois Central is well remembered for its extensive fleet of side-door cabooses constructed in the company's shops at Centralia, Illinois (see the photo shown on page 6). Overall they appeared much like the traditional cupola and end-platform caboose except that each had a small side door, used mainly by the conductor to lean out to check the train (as a sort of fresh-air bay-window) or "hoop" train orders being handed up to the passing train from

Proving that some railroads would go to great lengths to recycle surplus rolling stock into cabooses, Quebec's Cartier Railway created this caboose from a retired passenger baggage car. Aside from the obligatory bay window, the car features a hung side freight door. *Jim Mischke*

Following World War II, a number of railroads acquired U.S. Army troop sleepers made surplus by peacetime and used them in various capacities such as for housing maintenance-of-way workers or moving mail and express on passenger trains. Frugal New England carrier Bangor & Aroostook apparently got a good deal on a whole batch of troop sleepers, for they became the foundation for BAR's postwar caboose fleet. The road's Derby (Maine) shops rebuilt the cars, adding bay windows, enclosed end platforms with side doors, and appropriate crew facilities within. One of the interesting cars marches along at the end of the Searsport (Maine) local in 1974. *Mike Schafer*

station operators. A few other railroads had similar cabooses, but with larger side doors for handling LCL (less-than-carload) freight and incidental company shipments.

Post-construction customization was quite common, and one of the common alterations in later years was the blocking out of windows. Windows being inherently breakable, and railroads being inherently frugal, the "logical" solution to this problem was to blank out "nonessential" windows with plate steel. To railroad management, "non-essential" often meant all windows in the car save for the bay or cupola windows. After all, the crews were supposed to be doing paperwork or keeping watch on their

train when inside the cabooses, not gazing out at passing scenery.

As the photos in this chapter reveal, cabooses varied so wildly, even within a grouping, that they seemed to have personalities all their own. For example, there were thousands upon thousands of cupola cabooses over the years, but if you looked closely at each one, you'd see that they were more different than alike.

CHAPTER THREE

LIFE IN THE CABOOSE

As a career, railroading—especially during its high-profile heyday—had a perceived glamour and adventure to it that rivaled, say, life with the circus. (Some railroaders might claim there were a lot of parallels between the two.) What young boy or girl, at trackside with their folks in anxious anticipation of an approaching train, hasn't been enthralled by its passing. To look up at the engineer in charge of the locomotive, be it a fire-breathing behemoth of the steam era or a nine-thousand-horsepower trio of diesels of late twentieth century railroading, was to see yourself in that command. *Now* you knew what you wanted to be when you grew up.

But the show wasn't over. As the train itself passed by—and for our purposes, this will be a

As a Chicago-bound freight on the Chicago & North Western slows to a halt at West Chicago, Illinois, one of the crew members occupying the Union Pacific caboose prepares to alight while the other takes in some fresh air on a fine summer afternoon in 1977. Meanwhile, a local cyclist perhaps ponders what life is like working aboard a train. The "P" designation on the cupola indicates that this is a pool caboose. *Steve Smedley*

53

To youngsters at trackside, the chair in the cupola seemed almost throne-like. To caboose crews, it was probably just another fanny unfriendly railroad seat. Ancient castings and all, this was a "walkover" seat. If the caboose was moving in the opposite direction, you could just flip the seatback and be facing the right way. *Jeff Kehoe*

perched in the cupola and entice him to wave back to acknowledge your lowly presence. ("Why, being in the caboose must be an important railroad job too. Maybe I'll do *that* when I grow up.")

Most railroaders have railroading in their blood to one degree or another, and despite all the trials and tribulations of working for the rail industry, few—looking back on their storied careers—would probably trade it for another job. But the truth is that railroading often could be (and to a fortunately lesser degree still can be) a miserable job, fraught with danger, unthinkable working hours, unyielding management, and a smorgasbord of frustrating problems—weather, misrouted cars, broken "knuckles" (locomotive and car couplers, not necessarily the human variety), and ornery co-workers to name just a few.

As the nerve center of a train, the caboose is where many of those problems, along with the day-to-day work routine, came home to roost, largely on the shoulders of the conductor—the boss of the train. Small wonder there were so many caboose nicknames that reflected this: brain buggy, ape cage, throne room, etc.

Home Away From Home

For much of the first century of their existence, cabooses were very much a personal thing. Why? Because on most railroads the conductor was usually semi-permanently assigned to a specific caboose, and that caboose followed the conductor on his assignments. Generally, conductors held down a specific run for extended periods—maybe even years. Unless he was assigned to a local freight that went out and returned the same day, a run usually took the conductor and his brakeman and flagman (both of whom weren't necessarily assigned to the same train with the conductor every time though) away from home base for at least two and maybe three days. So, the caboose served as both the office and the home of the crew.

This arrangement was both a bane and a blessing for the railroad. It was a hassle in that the railroad had to switch the caboose off the train when it arrived at the division point where the

freight of leviathan length, with over a hundred cars whose billboard-size sides serve as a "Who's who" in the list of classic American railroads—anticipation swelled again as young eyes peered for the caboose. The sight of this rolling "house" served as a sort of dessert, concluding the feast of watching the train's passage. With a little luck and maybe some frenzied waving while jumping up and down, you'd catch the eyes of a crew member

With a piece of tin foil serving as a makeshift lampshade, a Davenport, Rock Island & North Western conductor makes out the wheel report. The valve at upper right on the end wall shows brake line air pressure—an important item for the conductor to keep tabs on. A sudden change in the pressure could indicate that the train has broken in two or, worse, is in the process of derailing. *Mike Schafer*

conductor went off duty, but the up side was that the railroad did not have to taxi the conductor and his crew to a hostelry nor did it have to pay to put the crew up for the night at a hotel or motel.

Like a home, assigned cabooses reflected the personalities of their "owners." Some conductors put down carpeting (and likewise admonished fellow crew members for tramping in with dirt on their boots); some even committed the unmanly act of putting up lace curtains on the windows in an effort to provide a touch of homeyness. Interiors were decorated with personal touches such as family photographs and calendars.

Which brings to mind a story involving one conductor's caboose on the Chicago, Rock Island & Pacific in the 1960s. A Rock Island official was giving a tour of the railroad's Silvis, Illinois, shop and yard facilities to a boy scout troop. They got to tour the shop buildings and were even treated to a

look at the innards of a diesel locomotive. The tour climaxed with the look at the inside of a caboose. The official merely unlocked the door to the crummy and told the boys to walk through, have a look, and come back out. They filed in on their own but were an awful long time in re-emerging. Finally, the perplexed official climbed up to see what was going on. He found out: The interior of the caboose was wallpapered with "girlie" pinups and *Playboy* centerfolds! Most of the scouts probably decided then and there that this indeed was the career they wanted to pursue.

The era of the assigned caboose was in twilight as the 1950s unfolded. It was becoming increasingly impractical and time-consuming to remove one caboose from the train and replace it with a fresh crew and caboose at every division point a cross-country train passed through. For example, a Santa Fe train traveling from Chicago to Los

Before the days of direct radio dispatching, one of the hazards of the job was having to snag or "hoop" train orders "on the fly" or while the train was in motion. The conductor of this Detroit, Toledo & Ironton/Ann Arbor freight passing through Carleton, Michigan, is about to snag the loop of string that holds his train orders. Adventurous though the process may look, it was not a pleasant task in sub-zero or rainy weather. Regardless of the elements, a sure footing was mandatory. *Mike Schafer*

Angeles went through nearly 20 crew changes and therefore as many caboose exchanges. This wasn't a big problem during the steam era when trains had to stop anyway at division points to have locomotives changed out, but after dieselization this was not the case—diesels could run through from Chicago to L.A. with only occasional (and brief) fueling stops. Logic changed. If locomotives could run through, so could cabooses, saving time and money spent on switching.

As American railroads became fully dieselized by the end of the 1950s, assigned cabooses became a target for management directly responsible for cost control. The result was a national movement toward caboose "pooling," which allowed railroads to assign any of their cabooses to the entire trip of any train. As a result, a single caboose on a Chicago-L.A. run might be used by nearly 20 different crews. In the space of a few years, the role of the caboose was transformed from someone's "home away from home" to a rolling Motel 6. Says the detraining crew to the new crew at a division point, "We'll leave the light on for ya."

Since this change directly involved a crew's working conditions, "pooling agreements" had to be negotiated between the railroads and the unions. Pooling took hold first on long-distance runs, and it was well into the 1970s before all caboose operations were so affected. The agreement was quite beneficial to railroads because it resulted in better caboose utilization and a big cost savings. Fewer cabooses were necessary to "protect" the same number of trains, and the railroads also saved on the costs associated with switching.

A Day At The Office

In the days before computers, the conductor himself was in many ways a "dispatcher"—a dispatcher for paper, that is, not trains. Indeed, paperwork could consume more than half of the conductor's time on the job. Such work kept the oil-fired caboose lamps glowing above the conductor's desk far into the night and good strong "caboose coffee" (see recipe elsewhere) simmering on the stove.

The conductor had three basic kinds of paperwork to deal with: train orders and clearance forms, waybills, and the wheel report. Clearance forms, issued by the dispatcher to a train's engineer and conductor, gave permission for the train to exist and venture out of the railroad. Train orders governed the specifics of the train's movement over the railroad in regard to other trains on the line. Generally, train orders were issued by the dispatcher to station operators along the route of a train, originally via telegraph and later via radio; the operators copied the train orders, in triplicate, onto special tissue paper ("flimsies") which were handed up to the engineer and conductor as the train passed the train-order station. Train orders dictated a host of instructions, but mainly they dictated where, on a single-track railroad, each train would pass trains going in either direction.

Though it occurred thousands of times daily throughout the American rail system before the advent of direct radio train control, the process of "handing up orders" was fascinating to watch. The operator had two sets of orders, one for the head-end crew in the locomotive and one for the caboose crew. Each set was tied together with a string and clipped to a train-order "hoop," which usually was a 'Y'-shaped stick. The loop of string encompassed the upper part of the Y, and the hoop was held up by the train operator standing as near the tracks as he or she safely dared. As the locomotive passed by, one of the crew leaned out to snag the loop of string bearing the train order. The procedure was repeated for the caboose crew. To snag the orders, the conductor usually stood on the rear steps of the caboose.

57

Perhaps more than anything, members of the caboose crew feared a derailment. Fate could land their crummy in a river, on its side down an embankment, or at the top of a heap of cars that derailed ahead of it. The rear-end crew of this Illinois Central Gulf freight was lucky. Although most of their train derailed, the last few cars and the caboose came to a stop before being pulled into the fray. The crew was shaken but unhurt. *Steve Smedley*

Since they were paramount to the safety of passengers and crews, train orders were in a sense the "word of God"—at least on the railroad (where the dispatcher might be considered to be very near that plane of deity)—and their abidance was absolute. So if either the locomotive or caboose crew somehow missed snagging the orders, the train had to be brought to a halt and the situation remedied. Once the orders were in hand, engineer and conductor had to study them to be absolutely clear on their meaning.

More mundane was the conductor's handling of waybills and wheel reports. On a freight train, every car except for the caboose usually had a waybill. The waybill indicated the car's owning railroad, shipper, contents, weight, consignee (the final receiver), routing, and anything else pertinent to invoicing. Waybills traveled with their respective cars from point of origin to point of destination. If the train stopped en route to take on more cars, then the conductor was responsible for securing their waybills. Likewise, for any cars set out during a run, the conductor had to make certain the corresponding waybills were delivered to the station agent or connecting railroad.

Requiring considerably more attention and pencil work was the wheel report, which listed the details of every car on the train: the car owner's initials and numbers, car contents and weight, and where the car was added to or set out from the train (if it wasn't traveling with the train for the whole trip). The wheel report thus provided a statistical record of the train from which the clerks back at headquarters could extrapolate charges and other billing information. Using the wheel report, the conductor could also determine the weight of the entire train (minus the locomotives) at any given point—an important consideration. A train exceeding the recommended tonnage limit could stall the engine(s) on even minor hills, delaying other trains and in general tying up the railroad.

Assembled from the wheel report, the switchlist provided the conductor with an agenda for efficient train switching. It showed where cars were to be set out and picked up en route and where all cars were going. At the final destination of the train, the switchlist—which had been updated by each conductor that had been assigned to the train throughout its journey—was passed on to switching-yard crews so that they knew how the cars should be redistributed to connecting trains or to local customers.

Other caboose crew members were hardly idle while the conductor was engrossed with sheaves of paper. The brakeman and flagman were required to maintain their watch on the moving train via the bay window or cupola, and to help with any switching maneuvers.

Caboose Cuisine

Cooking aboard a caboose was almost an art unto itself—and unfortunately it has become a lost art. The need for cooking abilities was high during the era when crews literally lived aboard cabooses for two or three days at a time during a round trip over the division. The need for culinary skills lessened as travel times were shortened and the number of eating establishments—"fast food" or otherwise—that were within a reasonable proximity of the railroad grew. Today it's not at all uncommon to see a freight train parked near a McDonalds or a well-known local "home cooking" restaurant with the crew heading for the lunch line.

Some restaurants are good, some are not so good, and such was the case with caboose cooking. As low person on the totem pole, the brakeman or flagman often was designated as Chief Cook & Bottlewasher unless the conductor had a penchant for cooking—and a few did. Otherwise, for the flagman it was baptism by fire: learn to cook or you and your fellow crew members would starve.

In an earlier era, mainline cabooses usually had ample refrigerator and storage space for foodstuffs. It took a lot of food to keep a crew of two or three well fed during the course of a two- or three-day round trip out of the home terminal. Crews were responsible for providing their own food, and they often did so with a respectable degree of creativity. Undoubtedly, a lot of produce was acquired surreptitiously, such as when a train had to make an "inspection stop" that coincidentally was adjacent to a farmer's cornfield—or even a chicken house. Fresh eggs for breakfast; fresh chicken for dinner.

Some crew members even came equipped with a shotgun or fishing tackle in hopes of tagging trackside delicacies like quail or snagging some bass or catfish from any creek bridges the train might happen to be stopped upon.

Chester "Chet" French, a longtime conductor on the Illinois Central Railroad, recalls his days living and working in cabooses: "The cooking came in various degrees of quality," he snickered. "The crew usually would buy groceries en route, and the flagman was usually chosen to prepare the food.

"We had one conductor, Fred Carrithers, I worked with in the late 1970s and early 1980s who had found an old Dutch oven at an antique shop. He put the contraption on top of the oil stove in the caboose and went to work. Of course, to make it work properly, we had to turn the oil stove up full bore; in the summertime this made the inside of the caboose unbearable, but it made for some great food—baked pork chops, potatoes, corn, and such. He could actually bake rolls—you know, the ones you get in a cardboard tube.

"On our run south [between Freeport and Clinton, Illinois], we'd eat dinner somewhere between Minonk and Bloomington before tying up for the night at Clinton. On our return trip the next morning, with a pot full of coffee, we'd always have more of the rolls he'd made the night before. Before we turned the stove down, we'd boil water and then do the dishes."

Chet went on to recall, "One Friday morning Carrithers prepared an excellent breakfast of eggs,

Cabooses would still be playing out their role for another quarter century when this tableau of American railroading was captured on film on the Wabash Railroad in September 1963. The caboose crew of eastbound symbol freight KD-4 (Kansas City-Detroit) waves at a bystander as it rolls by westbound Detroit-Kansas City freight ADK-1 in the passing siding at New Berlin, Illinois. *Dave Ingles*

bacon, and bread. Then he discovered his entire crew—who was staring lustfully at the big mound of bacon—was Catholic. He dipped his hand in some water and sprinkled it on the bacon. 'Swim, dangit, swim!' he said, blessing it into 'fish' so the guys could eat without guilt."

Hazards Of Caboose Life

By nature, cabooses could be quite dangerous. The most common problem involved slack action, which results during train braking or when a train moves over rolling terrain. Although an engineer can apply the locomotive and car brakes together, there is a sort of domino effect in the way the car brakes set up. The cars toward the front of the train

began slowing down before those to the rear. The result? The front of the train is stopping while momentum still has the back of the train heading toward Kalamazoo, or wherever. Until the braking action reaches the back of the train, the rear cars began bunching up against the cars that are stopping. In this case, the slack is rolling in, and the caboose is last to feel it as it slams against the car ahead of it.

The opposite happens when a train starts from a standstill. It is difficult for a locomotive or even a set of locomotives to start a long freight train at once. Rather, the locomotives will push back against the train just enough to bunch the slack, and then pull forward to start the train, one car at a time. This is the easy way to overcome the inertia of a standing

60

RECIPE FOR "CABOOSE COFFEE"

Take several fistfuls of ground coffee and toss them into a tall enamel coffee pot; fill with cold water. Let stand unheated for a couple hours, maybe even overnight. Bring to a boil several minutes before you're ready to serve. Pour and drink. Pour through strainer or cheesecloth if you don't want grounds in your cup. Not for the timid.

train. Unfortunately, this does not necessarily ensure a smooth start, as each car is suddenly thrust from 0 mph to 4-5 mph as the slack runs out. Consequently, the last car in the train often gets a pretty good snap. And in the era of cabooses, you know which car that was. (Passenger train cars are equipped with special coupling systems which virtually eliminate slack between cars, so slack action is negligible in passenger trains of reasonable length.)

In a similar vein, a train rolling over a line that follows a roller-coaster terrain is constantly subject to slack action as the train crests short hills and bottoms out in the valleys. An experienced engineer can minimize slack action with skilled manipulation of the throttle and train and/or locomotive brakes, using just enough braking action on the cars alone to "stretch" the train and keep the cars from bunching.

Crew members occupying the caboose always had to be alert for slack action, whether the train was standing or rolling. Usually they knew when it was coming, through radio communication with the engineer, by knowing the terrain they were in, and mostly by simply "feeling" the movement of the train. Slack was usually a two-part happening; first you'd feel the slack run in, and then you'd feel it run out. The rule of thumb is that if the slack runs in easy, it will run out hard and vice versa.

You can also anticipate slack action by ear. Slack action is readily audible, and crews in the caboose could hear it, like thunder getting closer, one car at a time but in super-quick succession. Crew members usually made it a point to be seated if they knew their train was about to start or stop, but sometimes it could catch them off guard and throw them to the floor—a particularly perilous situation if they were thrown from the perch high up in the cupola. Now you know why crews in the crummy appreciated engineers who were especially skilled at starting, running, and stopping a train.

Conductor Chet French recalled one particular engineer he worked with who was kind of a rough handler with a train. "When the train was moving less than about 10 mph and he had to stop it," Chet said, "he had a bad habit of doing so by applying only the engine brakes and letting the train crash against the engine to stop. Usually when we knew he was going to do this, we would bail off the caboose just before it crashed to a stop!"

Probably more than anything, the thought of an accident curdled the blood of caboose crew members. In a derailment or wreck, head-end crews could hope that their hefty locomotives could provide at least a modicum of armor protection, even if the locomotive overturned. The front ends of trains were more likely to be involved in a mishap, especially considering that there is no lack of motorists who fail to grasp the concept that trains have the right of way. But cabooses, by their nature as mere wood or metal boxes on wheels, were more vulnerable in any mishap that involved the rear of a train.

Most chilling among such disasters were rear-end collisions between two trains. Such an incident is graphically portrayed—albeit with expertly constructed large-scale models rather than real trains—in Cecil B. DeMille's *The Greatest Show on Earth*. This 1952 movie classic—a staple in the classic movie section of any well-stocked video rental store—fairly accurately demonstrates with goose-bumply horror what happens when two trains attempt to occupy the same space as the deadly result of a caboose crew unable to carry out their duties.

In the film, the Ringling Brothers-Barnum & Bailey circus train is running in two sections, both

With sights such as this along the route of Vermont's Green Mountain Railroad near Cuttingsville, Vermont, during the spring of 1984, the trials and tribulations of working in the caboose seemed a little more worthwhile. *Mike Schafer*

powered by steam locomotives; the first section comprises the "freight" of the circus movement—the circus equipment, tents, wagons, and animals—while the second section is made up of sleeping and commissary cars filled with circus performers and management. As was the tradition in that era, the second section of a train followed the first by no less than 10 minutes. In the event that the first section had to make an unexpected stop, the flagman in the caboose was required to immediately trot down the tracks with his flares and lanterns to "protect" his train's rear end. Theoretically, ten minutes gave the flagman enough time to get far enough down the tracks so that any following trains had enough distance in which to stop after seeing the flagman's stop signals if the trains were traveling on non-signaled track.

In the movie's spectacular climax, villains at trackside use flares to trick the first section into halting. As the train does this, you can hear the engineer whistling the special signal to the conductor and flagman that the train is stopping and that the flagman is to protect the rear of the train. Alas, the bad guys trounce the conductor and flagman descending from the caboose of the now-standing first section. The rest is movie history. Unaware of the plight of the first section, the second section rounds the curve and comes face to hind end with the first section and—too late—makes a valiant attempt at an emergency stop. The caboose is reduced to ten million toothpicks, to say little of the rest of the first section, by the thundering second-section locomotive, which derails while its passenger cars jackknife into the night landscape, maiming people and setting free a menagerie of lions and tigers and bears (oh my).

Although the circumstances of this staged accident were hardly commonplace, rear-end collisions per se were and are not at all unheard of. The most famous real-life accident of this nature occurred in the small hours of April 30, 1900, when Illinois Central's southbound *New Orleans Special*, the railroads fastest Chicago-to-New Orleans run—known locally as "The Cannonball"—plowed into the rear end of a standing freight train at Vaughan, Mississippi. As with Cecil B. DeMille's circus train disaster, the crew of the IC freight had somehow failed to protect the rear of their train which was in the process of entering a siding to clear for the Cannonball when it halted. On account of a reverse curve, Cannonball engineer John Luther "Casey" Jones was unable to see the standing freight until it was too late. Despite a heroic effort to stay with his engine to brake his speeding passenger train, the Cannonball made rubble of the freight's caboose and two boxcars, and Casey Jones went to his glory. Fortunately, no passengers were killed, and Casey became an indelible part of American railroad lore.

Such disasters were greatly alleviated by the automatic block signal, which came into widespread use during the World War I era. Block signals protect trains from following trains, flagman notwithstanding. Unfortunately for caboose crews, block signaling was not a universal solution to rear-end collisions since it was usually applied only to busy rail lines. On secondary lines that didn't have block signals—known as "dark" territory—the need for flagmen was still very real. Only with the widespread acceptance of radio communication after the 1960s between trains, between crew members of a train, and between train crews and the dispatcher was the need for flagmen gradually eliminated.

For both safety and cost considerations, the caboose was beginning to face extinction as the 1970s drew to a close. Life in the caboose had become pretty spartan anyway with the disappearance of assigned cars. You "checked in" to whatever caboose was on your train at the start of your work day, and you "checked out at the end" and took all your gear with you.

Railroading was entering a new era. In a world of ever-tightening cost controls, the caboose was a sitting duck, and life for the caboose was running out.

CHAPTER FOUR

RED AND
ANYTHING BUT

Red was the perfect color for cabooses. Bright and easy to see from afar, red is a color that alerts. Visually it spells possible danger, hence you have red stop signs (stop, here, NOW) and red fire engines (get out of the way NOW). Crews of red cabooses probably felt better knowing their little office—vulnerable at the end of a train—could be easily spotted by roving switch engines in a yard or by mainline trains approaching from behind. On a more aesthetic level, red is just plain well-liked as a color.

Before color photography emerged during the 1930s, the world seemed a black and white place. In a way it was. Although colors did abound in

Cabooses and the color red are almost synonymous, and red remained the favored caboose color throughout most of the 20th Century. But after mid-century, railroads began deviating from that norm—with a rainbow of results. This Toledo, Peoria & Western "caboose hop" at Pekin, Illinois, in 1992 carries two of the road's cabooses, one in more-or-less traditional red (but with a gray stripe) and the other a striking combination of four hues. *Steve Smedley*

65

One popular way to deviate from red was for railroads to apply their diesel paint scheme—or at least a close variation of it—to cabooses (unless the diesel scheme itself was red, of course). Green Burlington Northern diesels leading a Chicago-bound freight at La Crosse, Wisconsin, skim past the extended-vision caboose of a standing freight. Car ends were yellow to better reflect headlights of trains approaching from behind. *Mike Schafer*

everyday life, it wasn't quite to the range that they do now. The technology of color pigmentation was still its infancy. Sure, bright colors like yellow and orange were available, but brightly colored paints were quite expensive and not nearly as durable as tried-and-true dark browns, blacks, greens, and oxide reds.

U.S. railroads have long been notoriously frugal, so the vast majority of freight cars of the late

1800s and most of the twentieth century were painted in browns and "boxcar red," itself a color closer to brown than red. Any brightly colored, elaborately lettered "billboard" freight cars of the period usually belonged to meat-packers, brewers, and food producers—companies which were willing to spend the extra money required for more-expensive paint and lettering in return for the free

Denver & Rio Grande Western 01500 at Ogden, Utah, in 1969 wears the handsome color combination of Aspen Gold and silver worn not by Rio Grande's freight diesels but its passenger locomotives. *Mike Schafer*

advertising exposure to pedestrians and motorists who had to wait for the train to pass.

Bright red, of course, was a natural for cabooses because of the visibility factor, and though bright red paint was more expensive to apply, railroads justified the extra expense in the name of safety. Nonetheless, some eternally thrifty companies chose dark boxcar reds or browns for their cabooses.

With red as the ordained color of crummies for so many years, small wonder that red is the color the admiring public most often associates with cabooses. After World War II, though, this began to change—sometimes drastically—as cabooses began to show up in liveries that were departures from the "norm." Such revolution might be linked to dieselization as well as the

introduction of the streamlined passenger train, both of which began to catch on as the Depression was winding down late in the 1930s. Diesel locomotives and streamliners brought splashes of color to railroading, and railroads began to discover that color could be integral to corporate identification. Further, brightly colored paint was becoming more affordable and durable.

The dieselization period for American railroads extended from about 1939 to 1959. During and after that time, railroads became closely identified by the paint schemes worn by their locomotives and passenger cars, so for some lines the logical next step was to apply those liveries—or at least variations of them—to their cabooses as well. This was especially evident during the 1970s as

Early on, Illinois Terminal Railroad began applying its unusual lime green and yellow diesel colors to some of its cabooses, one of which is shown in Peoria, Illinois, in 1961. Because of the shape of the yellow areas, the railroad referred to this as its "football" scheme. *Leon Onofri*

Though not thought of as an overall bright, visible color combination, Erie Lackawanna's revered maroon/gray/yellow diesel scheme began showing up on cabooses as the 1970s unfolded. The cars wore the colors handsomely; yellow reflective Scotchlite reflective stripes enhanced their visibility. *David P. Oroszi*

more railroads began to think in terms of corporate identity, and by the end of the decade railroads everywhere were applying a universal paint scheme to all their locomotives and cabooses.

But not quite all of them. Far-flung Southern Pacific kept with reddish brown cabooses with orange ends (locomotives were gray and red). Latter-day Illinois Central abandoned red and went with a hard-to-see light gray with white lettering (freight diesels were black with white logos, lettering, and striping). Newly formed Norfolk Southern Corporation, for the short time it had cabooses, painted them traditional red rather than the mundane black worn by its diesels.

But the end result? A riot of caboose colors, in red and almost anything but.

Boston & Maine's "buggies"—as cabooses were known on the B&M—wore the road's black-and-blue scheme. Wearing a fresh coat of paint, one of the buggies totes along behind an eastbound freight at Greenfield, Massachusetts. *Howard Ande*

The common caboose paint scheme of the Chessie System railroads (Baltimore & Ohio, Chesapeake & Ohio, and Western Maryland following a 1972 amalgamation) was an adaptation of the diesel scheme: yellow and blue with orange trim. Locomotive and caboose are at Cumberland, Maryland, in 1977. *Don Jilson*

Chesapeake & Ohio (C&O) 903103 utilized the traditional Chessie System caboose colors (previous photo) but flip-flopped, with the orange as the dominate color and yellow as trim. The unusual scheme was photographed in Indianapolis in 1982. *Jim Mischke*

ABOVE AND RIGHT
Pennsylvania Railroad 478134, built in 1951, wears PRR's familiar Tuscan Red (used primarily on the road's passenger equipment, as seen in the background) but with a yellow cupola. This style of caboose on the Pennsy was known as a Class N8; it is shown in 1963. When Conrail was formed in 1976, it acquired large amounts of former-PRR equipment, including many cabooses, which got painted in Conrail blue and white as illustrated by the N8-class caboose about to cross the Great Miami River in Dayton, Ohio, in 1977. *PRR photo, John Dziobko; CR photo, David P. Oroszi*

Richmond, Fredericksburg & Potomac diesels were dark blue and gray, but the road chose a lighter blue for some of its cabooses, such as the 940 at Alexandria, Virginia, in 1968. *C .G. Parsons, Thomas Hoffmann collection*

No color: Kansas City Southern experimented by leaving its aluminum-walled cabooses *au naturel*, applying only red trim and numbers and the yellow/red KCS emblem. *Jim Mischke*

Soo Line Railroad, owned by Canadian Pacific Railway (note the "CP RAIL SYSTEM" stenciled in the lower left bolster frame of the car), experimented with a brown and white livery for some of the cabooses it still operates. The scheme was not particularly well-received, and some recent caboose repaintings on the Soo Line have revived the white, red, and black scheme that the railroad had been using on its equipment for some 30 years. *Shane Amundson*

The Gateway Western Railway, operating between Kansas City and St. Louis, seems to have decided on a paint-scheme pattern, but not which colors should be used. Regardless, bystanders won't have any problem identifying what railroad owns these International extended-vision cabooses! *Scott Muskopf*

Author's favorite: The New York, Chicago & St. Louis Railroad—Nickel Plate—was known for its fleet of short, fast freight trains serving Chicago, St. Louis, Buffalo, Cleveland, Pittsburgh, and other important Midwest cities. The road, merged out of existence in 1964, made no bones about its claim to fame: Emblazoned across the top of nearly every one of its bright red cabooses was "NICKEL PLATE HIGH SPEED SERVICE." Seeing one of these classic cabooses on a passing freight underscored the excitement and mystique of railroading. *Mike Schafer*

Increased safety awareness during the 1980s led some railroads to apply safety-theme paint schemes to their locomotives and rolling stock. Operation Lifesaver, a safety campaign of national scope shepherded by the Association of American Railroads, plays prominent in this caboose belonging to CSX Transportation, successor to Chessie System and other Southeastern carriers. *R. B. Olson, Thomas Hoffmann collection*

CHAPTER FIVE

THE CABOOSE FALLS FROM GRACE

Cabooses were their own worst enemy. They represented a major capital expense, especially for a large railroad requiring hundreds of cabooses. They became costly to operate and maintain, and inherently they could be dangerous for train crews. On railroad rosters, cabooses were classified as "non-revenue" equipment; that is, they did not generate any transportation revenues. Rather, they were part of the cost of doing business.

The penchant for cost-cutting on U.S. railroads is legendary, so the more expensive it became to acquire, operate, and maintain cabooses, the more they became a target for railroad accountants. At the

As the twentieth century waned and American railroads entered a period of unparalleled modernization and growth, the caboose became an unfortunate (for reasons of aesthetics, anyway) victim in the name of progress. But like those which have passed on before it—the steam locomotive, small-town wooden depots, and semaphore signals—the caboose remains an icon of railroading that will not be forgotten. (Lamoille Valley Railroad, 1981.) *Mike Schafer*

Owatonna, Minnesota, July 1976. It could be Anyplace, U.S.A., in a time when most towns worth their names still had a wooden railroad depot with semaphore train-order signals and a real, live station agent. Freight trains, such as this westbound Chicago & North Western run heading for Pierre, South Dakota, still carried cabooses (or way-cars or cabins or crummies, depending on the locale or individual railroad) for housing the conductor, brakeman, and flagman. But the 1970s were the last hurrah for the caboose. A decade later, everything in this scene had vanished, save for the freight train itself—sans caboose. *Steve Glischinski*

same time, the need for cabooses was being chipped away by technology. Chief among such was, of course, the computer. Paperwork that once required a generous desktop, a meticulous, patient conductor, and hours of time could now be spit out in a fraction of the time by a computer-wielding clerk at railroad headquarters. Now, instead of writing wheel reports, updating waybills, and creating switchlists, the conductor was simply handed a set of computer printouts to which he or she only needed to make quick reference when switching the train.

The jobs of brakemen and flagmen were likewise affected by electronics. The almost-overnight

widespread acceptance of the automatic hotbox detector during the 1980s in a sense replaced the cupola (or bay window) and the watchful eye of a crew member on lookout. Hotbox detectors are positioned at trackside; they are not on-train devices. Located at strategic intervals along railroad main lines, hotbox detectors are equipped with sensors that can detect both overheated bearings and dragging equipment—brake or coupler rigging that may have worked its way loose. As a train passes a detector, it counts and "reads" the axles and then via radio issues a robotic computerized voice that confirms to the crew and dispatcher "no defects," or alerts them that one of the axles on the train may have a problem or that something is dragging.

Radio is hardly a new technology in American life, yet its refinements since World War II have also spelled doom for the caboose. In modern railroading, radios are compact, reliable, and—thanks to trackside microwave towers—have much greater long-range capabilities. Radios provide instant communication between train crews and dispatchers and other train crews. If a train should have to come to an unexpected halt or if there is a mishap, the crew can immediately contact the dispatcher and other nearby train crews via radio to be on the alert for potential problems. Thus radios, in conjunction with automatic signaling systems, have virtually eliminated the need for a flagman to protect a stopped train.

Lots of people in this modern world have been replaced by so-called "black boxes"—the catch-all term for any technological wonder (usually electronic) that theoretically can do a job formerly done by humans. Black boxes help sort mail at the post office; they answer telephones and take orders and messages; they diagnose an automobile engine. On a railroad, black boxes automatically lower crossing gates for approaching trains—a job that for more than a century was done by gatemen. Where a tower man once controlled traffic at an intersection of two railroads lines, a black box now performs the task. Eventually a black box known as an "EOT" or "ETD" (end-of-train device) or "FRED" (flashing rear-end device) served as the final death knell for the caboose.

This telemetry invention, small enough to fit in a musical-instrument box, had its humble beginning on the Florida East Coast Railway in 1969. Strikebound from 1963 to 1971 over a controversial battle with unions regarding pay increases, FEC was an early aggressor in reducing the costs of crews and train operation. Whereas three- to five-man crews were required on trains of most other Class I railroads, FEC began running them with two-man crews, which in part led to the elimination of cabooses. The telemetry device pioneered by FEC, used on the last car of a freight train, could indicate air-brake pressure at the rear of the train and transmit the reading via radio to equipment in the locomotive cab that could receive, decode, and display the transmission to the locomotive crew. Any problem in the train's air-brake line such as a break-in-two (when a train accidentally uncouples while running) or a damaged air hose could be recognized in the transmission. The success of this new "black box" permitted FEC to eliminate cabooses in 1972.

In David-and-Goliath fashion, the victor in the confrontation between cabooses and advancing technology was this little electronic box, known variously as an EOT or ETD (end-of-train device) or FRED (flashing rear-end device). Mounted on the trailing coupler of the last car of a train, ETDs—equipped with a flashing light to warn following trains—transmit information to the locomotive crew regarding brake line pressure and other vital signs. *Steve Smedley*

For ten years FEC was a proving ground for the inevitable. In the fall of 1982, the United Transportation Union (UTU) and most U.S. railroads reached a compact that allowed railroads to begin phasing out cabooses, replacing them with ETDs. Even with this sweeping mandate, four states—Montana, Nebraska, Oregon, and Virginia—passed laws (since repealed) requiring cabooses on all freight

These Norfolk Southern cabooses lying in mournful solitude in a scrap yard in 1991 are about to suffer the same fate that befell most of the thousands of cabooses that once roamed American rails from coast to coast. *Steve Smedley*

trains operating with in the state borders. Nonetheless, the caboose was running on borrowed time.

The argument against crummies had been mounting. Even with safety appliances like cushioned underframes and seatbelts, crews would be first to admit that slack action was still a major concern in safe caboose operation—and probably would be as long as there were cabooses. At the same time, studies and reports also indicated significantly fewer job-related accidents on cabooseless trains.

The economics of caboose operation was perhaps an even larger factor. With new cabooses costing as much as $80,000 apiece in the mid-1980s, railroads were blanching at the thought of having to replace old ones. To a large railroad which might have over a thousand cabooses, that could represent a considerable capital expenditure. To replace all the cabooses that were still operating on American railroads as the 1980s got under way would have cost nearly $1 billion.

And then there was the cost of operating a caboose. One major American railroad estimated that it cost nearly 70 cents per mile to operate a caboose, or about $1,300 per trip. Even adding or removing a caboose at the end of its run had a cost (about $30). Industry giant Burlington Northern (now Burlington Northern Santa Fe) estimated that it spent $36,000 operating and maintaining each of the 1,120 cabooses it had on its property in the mid-1980s.

Although labor unions and railroads had in 1982 agreed in principle to sanction the demise of the caboose, the UTU—citing the sensitive issue of safety—resisted the change. Arguing that there was nothing better than cabooses staffed by real humans to properly monitor train operation, some UTU members mounted campaigns aimed at

85

Caboose in twilight: One of Santa Fe's classics, trailing hot intermodal train No. 199 en route from Chicago to the West Coast, heads off into the sunset on a pleasant May evening in 1985 at Chillicothe, Illinois. *Steve Smedley*

state governments, asking them to pass laws forbidding cabooseless trains. The noble argument certainly appeared valid but turned out to be difficult to prove, as a number of railroads had been operating millions of cabooseless train-miles without major incidents.

Part of this could perhaps be attributed to the fact that ETDs and FREDs had become even more sophisticated since their introduction in 1969. Today's "smart FREDs"—smart in that they perform a number of tasks—operate on rechargeable batteries. They feature HVMs (Highly Visible Marker lamps) and monitor brake line pressure, signaling the engine crew at regular intervals if everything is normal and immediately if it isn't. They also indicate if the rear of the train is moving or not; whether the FRED's flashing light is on; and if the battery that runs the whole system is maintaining power.

Not surprising, the cost of operating FREDs is dramatically less—about half the cost of operating a caboose, according to the Association of American Railroads. And the capital investment is nil compared to $80,000 per new caboose. It appears the biggest drawback of the ETD might be aesthetics. There's just nothing like a caboose at the end of a train. Romanticists (which probably includes most of us reading this book) cannot put a price on aesthetics, but railroads can and did—and it was too much to pay.

CHAPTER SIX

Epilogue

In the mid-1920s some 34,000 cabooses roamed U.S. rails. That was the peak, and the number dwindled since. In 1937 the figure had dropped to about 32,000; by 1950, about 25,000; in 1960, just over 18,000; in 1970; about 14,000.

In the mid-1980s, some 12,000 crummies were hanging on for dear life, but the handwriting was on the (caboose) wall. The 1990s brought an almost total wipeout of an institution that had been around for almost 150 years. As of the mid-1990s, there were only a few hundred active cabooses on U.S. rails.

What happened to them? Where did they go? Are any cabooses still operating as intended? The answer to the first question is that this morning you probably drove to work in a car which was

Decorated caboose 275 of the Chicago & Illinois Midland Railroad, on display at what was the railroad's depot in Pekin, Illinois, contributes to the town's festive spirit during the 1995 Christmas holiday season. The depot is now used by a non-railroad concern; the railroad, whose main line was still active through Pekin, sold the caboose to an individual who thankfully kept the car painted in C&IM colors to comemmorate the decades-old carrier. *Steve Smedley*

Retired cabooses make dandy "buildings." This former Chicago, Burlington & Quincy caboose, sans wheels, was serving as Burlington Northern's yard office in Fort Madison, Iowa, when photographed in 1974. *Dave Ingles*

made of steel that—yup—once was a cupola, bay-window section, wall, or what-have-you part of a caboose. In short, most of the tens of thousands of cabooses that have existed since their inception in the early 1800s have been scrapped.

But cabooses are not quite extinct. Indeed, as this volume goes to press, a number of railroads still use cabooses, albeit in limited application. Several railroads—or at least labor unions—feel that cabooses are still necessary on runs that require a lot of switching maneuvers or long back-up moves. Backing up a train can be safer with a caboose leading the move. The conductor stands on the rear platform of the car to watch for obstructions on the track (chief among them, automobiles) that the engineer, many cars forward, might not be able to see. Since the

conductor can actually stop the train by using the brake valve on the caboose, the caboose becomes a safety enhancement.

Several railroads kept a few of their cabooses for purposes of recycling. For example, cabooses are ideal candidates for conversion into maintenance-of-way rolling stock for housing crews or work equipment. The Wisconsin Central Railroad, a relatively new (1987) regional railroad, owns but a handful of cabooses—none of which are used in the traditional caboose manner. One is on display along a freeway near the railroad's hub at Fond du Lac, Wisconsin, simply to denote WC being one of the city's largest employers. The remaining cabooses serve as unusual remote-control cars (see photo).

If you want to see cabooses in their original, "pure" form, your best bet is the local railroad

The Loram Company, which provides rail maintenance services for U.S. railroads, purchased surplus cabooses for its work trains. This bay-window caboose received several visible modifications, notably the special roof-mounted platform. The caboose is serving as part of a rail-grinding train working on the Southern Pacific main line near Colfax, California, in 1990. *Brian Solomon*

In an unusual twist, the Wisconsin Central Railroad used cabooses to reduce the number of crew members needed to operate certain trains. Railroad shop forces converted eight former Algoma Central cabooses into remote-control vehicles. Equipped with locomotive air-braking equipment and a radio receiver, the cars—coupled to a locomotive and linked via special plug-in cables—can be used to remotely operate the locomotive. Thus, an engineer can also serve as his train's brakeman, throwing switches and uncoupling cars while controlling his locomotive from trackside. Modified, the cabooses feature their own horns and headlights; the colored lights on the sides of the cupola provide an indication to the trackside operator whether the locomotive is in braking or acceleration mode. *C. E. Newton*

museum. Over the years, railroads have donated hundreds of retired cabooses to railroad museums throughout North America. Many museums have made painstaking efforts to restore the cars to their original appearance, and at museums and tourist railroads that feature operating trains, the public often can ride in cabooses. Similarly, numerous railroad aficionados have purchased cabooses, moved them onto a parcel of land (perhaps even the back yard), and applied some tender loving care to return them to authentic condition.

The number of cabooses that have been reincarnated into new, completely different lives is nothing short of amazing. In the 1970s and 1980s, as cabooses were being retired at an alarming rate, they could be had for next-to-nothing sums—save for the expense of moving one, which sometimes was more than the cost of the caboose itself—and companies and towns everywhere snatched them up. Suddenly, cabooses popped up everywhere but on active rails, serving as chambers of commerce, visitors' centers, gift shops, mini-museums . . . the possibilities were unlimited. Near the tourist mecca of Lake Geneva in southern Wisconsin, a string of cabooses serve as rooms at a motel complex, and at railroad-theme restaurants that have moved into former railroad depots throughout America; cabooses make for nifty private dining-room

Frisco caboose 1144 does double duty as the Frisco (Texas) Chamber of Commerce and the Bicentennial Steel Wheel Museum. No more long trips for this car, since the track on which it sits is shorter than the car. *Thomas Hoffmann*

The Chicago, Rock Island & Pacific Railroad perished in 1980, but much of its locomotives and rolling stock was adopted by others. The new life of this Rock Island caboose was as an office for a golf driving range in Bettendorf, Iowa. *Steve Smedley*

This Canadian Pacific wooden cupola caboose has been handsomely restored, but when photographed at Gananoque, Ontario, in 1982 it was serving as the park district office—not as an office of a CP freight. *C. W. Newton*

annexes. This writer's barber snips away at customers' locks in a barber shop housed in a former Illinois Central side-door caboose.

In other instances, cabooses have been acquired by a town or city and given a place of honor on city property wearing their original railroad livery simply to commemorate the railroad's importance to the community. Such is a fitting tribute to the importance of the railroad in building America.

Cabooses are largely gone from day-to-day railroading, but thanks to their one-time sheer numbers and the interest of private parties and even public concerns, people everywhere can still enjoy this nearly vanished icon of American ingenuity.

INDEX